get offa my case!

get offa my case!

GODLY PARENTING OF AN ANGRY TEEN

RICK HORNE

Shepherd Press
Wapwallopen, Pennsylvania

Get Offa My Case!
© 2012 by Rick Horne

Trade Paperback ISBN: 978-1-936908-14-1

eBook ISBN
Mobi format: ISBN 978-1-936908-15-8
ePub format: ISBN 978-1-936908-16-5

Published by Shepherd Press P.O. Box 24, Wapwallopen, Pennsylvania 18660

Page design and typesetting by Lakeside Design Plus
Cover design by Tobias' Outerwear for Books

First Printing, 2012
Printed in the United States of America

VP   23 22 21 20 19 18 17 16 15 14 13 12
14 13 12 11 10 9   8   7   6   5   4   3   2   1

Library of Congress Cataloging-in-Publication Data
Horne, Rick.
    Get offa my case! : Godly parenting of an angry, defiant teen / Rick Horne.
        p. cm.
    ISBN 978-1-936908-14-1 (trade pbk. : alk. paper)—ISBN 978-1-936908-15-8 (mobi ebook edition)—ISBN 978-1-936908-16-5 (epub ebook edition)
        1. Parent and teenager—Religious aspects—Christianity. 2. Parenting—Religious aspects—Christianity. 3. Parenting—Religious aspects—Christianity. 4. Child rearing—Religious aspects—Christianity. 5. Anger—Religious aspects—Christianity. I. Title.
    BV4529.H45 2011
    248.8'45—dc23
                                                                        2011025974

eBook Coupons
Free eBook for the purchaser of *Get Offa My Case!* in Paperback format
Go to: http://www.shepherdpress.com/ebooks
Mobi file for Kindle: CaseM01
ePub file for iPad: **Case01**

To Wayne and Carol Mack, Art and Ruth Nazigian,
Ken and Willie Tanis
A godly pastor and his wife who mentored Betty and me
as husband and wife and dad and mom to our six kids.
And two godly heads of schools and their wives
who encouraged me to grow during thirty-five years
of youth counseling in two Christian school settings.

CONTENTS

ACKNOWLEDGMENTS

The Lord specializes in getting water out of a rock, feeding many with a few loaves and fishes, changing plain water into rich wine and transforming hateful enemies into agents of peace. Whatever usefulness there is in this book comes because of the powerful work of the Holy Spirit to do all these things with the impervious, the inadequate, the unremarkable and the adversarial—me.

He uses lots of agents to extract value from weak sources. In the case of this book, the Lord has used all the members of my family, especially my wife, Betty, the rich counsel from the brothers and sisters at Christ Liberation Fellowship, our church, and the encouragement from other brothers and sisters who have walked with us through some of the rough waters and threatening mine fields of living with an angry teen.

Many thanks go to the folks at Shepherd Press for their encouragement to write this companion to my first book, *Get Outta My Face!,* for parents who love, and want to communicate with, their angry teens. This book picks up where that book left off, helping parents to hold their angry or defiant teen accountable when they don't want to communicate. Editing professional, Geoffrey Stone, guided me into better ways to organize, balance and express many of the concepts here. Similarly, I've received many words of encouragement to pursue this topic from Christian workers, pastors and parents who have struggled with an angry teen of their own.

My prayer is that the Lord may use this offering as thirst-quenching water, hunger-satisfying loaves and fishes, delight-producing sweet wine and family-enriching peaceable fruit. Most importantly, though, may he use it to glorify himself and make readers more satisfied with him. "You have made him glad with the joy of your presence" (Psalm 21:6). "The LORD is my chosen portion and my cup; you hold my lot. The lines have fallen for me in pleasant places; indeed, I have a beautiful inheritance" (Psalm 16:5–6).

SO, WHAT'S A CHRISTIAN PARENT TO DO?

"I'm so tired of living in this prison! If I have to be in by nine, I'm leaving. Nobody else's parents treat them like you treat me. Tom's mom said I could come and live with them if I want to. And if you lock the door like you said, then I'm outta here. I don't care. I'll do what I want to do when I want to do it. You can't make me do anything. Just get offa my case!"

Living with an angry, defiant teenager will drain the peace and sense of safety from any home. Most seriously, for the Christian parent, godly parenting with spiritual, mental and emotional balance becomes as difficult as trying to keep your footing in the ocean when the waves are rough. On the one hand the waves keep pounding the top half of your body as they roll toward the shore; at the same time you have to fight the strong undertow that is dragging your legs out from under you. In this book I'm going to use this rough seas metaphor because it can help us think about the rough waves of opposition and anger from our teens and the threatening undertow of our temptations to anger and fear and feelings of frustration that may emerge from our own hearts. Both, if left unchecked, will fill our homes with turmoil, fear, and pain and will undermine our godly parenting desires.

Sue's sophomore daughter is as big as she is. When Tina comes home from school she smells like cigarette smoke, doesn't talk to her mother, sequesters herself in her room and won't answer Sue when she calls her or asks her a question. If Sue tries to correct Tina or asks her what she is doing or where she's been, her daughter yells at her to "mind your own f****** business." Sue's own spiritual balance takes a big hit during these times. She's tempted to yell back at her daughter, to threaten Tina and even use some of the same foul language in her own anger. Sue has spent many restless hours worrying, feeling frustrated and defeated, and sometimes just wishing Tina would just leave. Home is much more pleasant when Tina is not there, but worry also nags at Sue when Tina is away. Sue's unsettledness and the unhappiness at home drains her energy and leads her to distraction. She finds it hard to focus clearly on the needs of Tina's brother and sisters, keep her balance with other family needs and even to concentrate during her quiet time with the Lord. The "fight" never ends. Keeping her footing in these rough waters is hard.

Maintaining stability in a home with an angry teenager is no easy task. The constant pounding and unpredictable waves created by a defiant and disrespectful teen bombard us within and without. Our attitudes and reactions, like an undertow, throw us off balance from within. The sinfulness of our own hearts directs our angry reactions in ways that can drag us into saying and doing things that only make the problems worse.

The intensity of a teen's angry attitudes, words and actions can be intimidating. In addition to the turbulence she creates in the home, there is also the real possibility that she will do some irreversible damage to herself or others. In the face of threats to run away, destroy something or hurt someone or herself, we may be terrified that our child might do what they threaten to do. The threats could be realistic because we may have seen them become more and more bold with angry outbursts, take increasingly dangerous risks or do physical damage to our home. Their rage can be violent. We've encountered their tirades when they haven't liked us trying to hold the line on correct standards of behavior. *So what's a Christian parent to do?*

The Most Important Question

This is an important question, but it's not the first one we must ask ourselves if we are going to meet this turbulence in a godly way. The question we must begin with is *What's a Christian parent to be like in these difficult situations?* This question is the subject of Part 1 and focuses on how parents can keep their footing in spite of the force of external waves of rebellion. It addresses the fierce undertow of responses that threaten to emerge from our own hearts and will compound our home problems. Solomon's wisdom is critical to heed here: "Keep (or *guard* in the NIV) your heart with all vigilance, for from it flow the springs of life" (Proverbs 4:23). By keeping or guarding our hearts in these times, we will be able to keep our footing in rough waters. We will find the courage we need to persevere righteously and the hope we need to experience the peace, joy and love of Christ—even while the waves keep pounding against us.

In Part 2, I talk about specific, strategic biblical counsel that parents need to bring to bear on their angry, defiant teen. The aim of this conversation will be to show him respect in a way he's probably not experienced. This will move him into the deep, threatening waters of accountability. He probably won't want to go there willingly, but your respectful approach to him is going to drag him there anyway. Such counsel will help you address the waves of anger and threats of violence or defiance that come at you, and to make that turbulence something that your teen will feel. You will walk alongside as a dad who has come to understand more of his biblical parenting identity and his son's young adult identity, a father who works to show biblical respect to his son. This discussion drags his son to an intimidating, even frightening, place. This discussion has the effect of a riptide on an ocean swimmer; it is a quiet, powerful current that draws his son into threatening, deep waters where he does not want to go on his own.

In Part 3, I talk about specific biblical actions you can take to let your teenager sink in the threatening, deep waters of accountability. It is these that we pray God may use to motivate our child to make cooperative, respectful and responsible choices—ultimately for the right reasons. He's been bringing the pounding waves of troubledness and discomfort into your home for some time. Now you are going to make it evident that this problem of troubledness and discomfort is for him to bear, not you and the rest of the family. He's been handing you the problem for some time, now you will learn how to give him the problem while maintaining a spirit of grace and love. You will learn how to use the biblical resources at your disposal to let him feel the weight of his uncooperative, disrespectful decision-making, but always in the context of Christ's love. You are going to let your teen sink in over his head. You are going to let him gasp. He won't drown, but God willing and with the Spirit's intercession, like the prodigal son, who "came to himself" (Luke 15:17), this deep water will humble him and motivate him to cry out for help.

Part 4 is largely autobiographical. Our heavenly Father took my wife, Betty, and me through a stormy sea with one of our six teens. We experienced the pounding waves of his outbursts and the sinful reactions of our own hearts. This part shows you how to grasp the rich resources that your Father in heaven makes available to you when you "pass through the waters" (Isaiah 43:2). It shows you how to make him your delight in the midst of your storm while letting your teen sink in deep water that is over his head so that he, by God's grace, will call out for help.

One final note about Part 4: My children have all read this section, especially my son, Jed, through whom our Father has been teaching Betty and me to be more like Christ and to be more and more content with Christ. All our kids, including Jed and his wife, have given permission to write about these home experiences from years past. We're all still sinners. That won't be resolved till we see the Savior face to face. But the friendships that we all now share and the enjoyment we are able to have in Christ after those years of rough waters are a tribute to God's grace and a testimony to his power.

May our good and gracious Father use this book to give you enjoyment in Christ and make him your heart's desire for the peace of God in your relationship with your difficult teen.

PART 1

KEEPING YOUR FOOTING IN ROUGH WATERS

Fear not, for I have redeemed you. . . . When you pass through the waters, I will be with you; and through the rivers, they shall not overwhelm you. . . . For I am the LORD your God, the Holy One of Israel, your Savior.

—Isaiah 43:1–3

Jesus said, "In the world you will have tribulation. But take heart; I have overcome the world" (John 16:33). Opposition did not surprise him. He does not want it to surprise us either, even when such opposition might be found in our homes: "A person's enemies will be those of his own household" (Matthew 10:36). When anger erupts, Jesus makes it clear that it is not always provoked by our unrighteous parenting. Of course it can arise in our homes because we have set the stage for it by some of our own parenting patterns, but that is often not the case. "Everyone who does wicked things," Jesus asserts, "hates the light and does not come to the light, lest his works should be exposed" (John 3:20). Such hatred can come at us from the culture outside our homes and from the heart of an angry teen inside our homes.

> What comes out of a person is what defiles him. For from within, out of the heart of man, come evil thoughts, sexual immorality, theft, murder, adultery, coveting, wickedness, deceit, sensuality, envy, slander, pride, foolishness. All these evil things come from within, and they defile a person.
>
> —Mark 7:20–23

Godly parenting in a sea of rough water is what this book is about. How can we keep our balance and stability in a home with the turbulence of an angry teen? In Part 1, I look at four resources, or foundational supports: God's glory, his promises, his Word, and prayer. God has given us these supports to brace ourselves and remain stable *in* rough water. These will give us stability and shore up our own hearts for the important next steps that we must take with our angry teen. Our commitment to these four supports will guarantee that our homes will be places where God's name is honored and his grace is displayed through us—regardless of our teen's disposition.

We must not rush past these supports. Just as contractors must pay careful attention when pouring the foundation of a home, we must be careful to build a strong foundation in our own hearts. Some of the recent earthquakes in Japan, Haiti, Indonesia, the Philippines, India and China remind us that a good foundation is critical for standing firm in an earthquake—or against pounding waves. Likewise it's important that our lives are built on strong supports in order to weather the storms in our homes. It's not enough to just *do* the right thing with your angry teen. The "right" steps or the "right" words will not be the silver bullet you need to bring peace and harmony to your home. You must *be* the right person doing the right things to experience God's peace in your home. Part 1 provides you with the foundational supports you need to make the important decisions to which God directs you with your teen.

When God is glorified, all of him is glorified. That means the wonderful grace that characterizes him pours from him in Christ and swells around us and in us because he is a gracious God. His gracious provision of himself will motivate you to "stand" (see Ephesians 6:13–14) and "keep you from stumbling" (Jude 24). His loving promises will encourage you, his Word will instruct you and prayer will position and empower you.

1

KEEPING YOUR FOOTING AS GOD'S GLORY MOTIVATES YOU

Be exalted, O God, above the heavens! Let your glory be over all the earth!

—Psalm 57:5

In John 11, Jesus entered a situation that has some similarities to home settings shown in this book. There are some clear differences, but the emotions, thoughts, temptations and maybe some of the words are similar to the ones that your teen is experiencing or has expressed and that may threaten to overwhelm you as well.

Mary and Martha experienced loss. Their brother had died. They were overwhelmed with deep grief for four days. They believed that Lazarus would not have died if Jesus had been present. Some of their words seem to be a mixture of resentment and hope. They had obviously talked to each other about the crisis and in their grief came to the same conclusion about Jesus' absence. When Jesus arrived at their home in Bethany, he met each sister separately, and each one said the same thing to him. Martha said, "Lord, if you had been here, my brother would not have died" (John 11:21). Just a few verses later, Jesus also met Mary in her grief. She said exactly the same thing when she saw him (see verse 32). They had hope in the resurrection at the last days, but they felt hopeless about their immediate loss. They assumed that nothing in the present could bring back their brother.

Like Mary and Martha we experience fear, confusion and a sense of hopelessness in dealing with our angry, defiant teen. We fear for our son's safety and his and our other children's spiritual and emotional well-being. Our own sins may compound the anxiety we are feeling. We might be ashamed because turbulence is erupting in our "Christian family," guilty because of doubts about our parenting skills and worried that reproach will be brought on Christ because the Christian teachings we've tried to apply haven't worked as we thought they should. All these are common reactions of Christian parents in a home with an angry or out of control teen.

Our teen may have some things in common with Mary and Martha too. She may have experienced a great loss or be deeply saddened by a turn of events in her life that seems to last forever (though, maybe in real time, it has only lasted a few hours or, perhaps, days). She may think that her parents have arbitrary and ridiculous expectations and demands, which she believes will never change.

In the midst of the rough water in which Mary and Martha stood, Jesus showed up and directed their hearts and minds to the first truth to which they needed to commit: that God would be glorified in this difficult situation. This hope would be their source for stability in the midst of their immediate fear and present sense of loss, as well as the work of God in the future.

When Jesus first heard of Lazarus' sickness, he said, "This illness does not lead to death. It is for the glory of God, so that the Son of God may be glorified through it" (John 11:4). Later, at the gravesite, Jesus said to Mary and Martha, "Did I not tell you that if you believed you would see the glory of God?" (v.40). From the outset, Jesus knew that there were going to be waves of confusion, grief, misunderstandings and doubts that would arise because of Lazarus' death. The counsel Jesus gave the disciples and Mary and Martha in order to keep their footing during this crisis was to hope in "the glory of God."

Nothing is more sufficient for us when we feel threatened by our angry teen than the hope that God's glory will be displayed through the stormy waves that are rolling upon us and our household. The believer's passion and delight is to see God glorified. Our temptation, though, is to be like Peter who began to sink in the Sea of Galilee after Jesus told him to walk on the water toward him. He became concerned with himself, took his eyes off Jesus and looked at the stormy wind and waves (see Matthew 14:28–30). That's when he lost his footing.

Later in the book I'll direct our attention to what practical things you can and should do in these settings to address your teen's anger. But first we need to keep our eyes on Jesus and God's glory.

Satisfaction with God's Glory Gives Stability during Personal Attacks

When Saul was threatening and chasing David, he took refuge in God and found stability in resting in God's glory.

> In you my soul takes refuge; in the shadow of your wings I will take refuge, till the *storms of destruction* pass by. I cry out to God Most High, to God who fulfills his purpose for me. . . . Be exalted, O God, above the heavens! Let your glory be over all the earth! . . . My heart is steadfast.
>
> —Psalm 57:1–2, 5, 7

Stability was the practical outworking of entrusting himself to God's purpose of glorifying himself in the midst of his troubles. By focusing on God's glory David gained a firm footing during his "storms of destruction." He declared, "My heart is steadfast, O God, my heart is steadfast!" (v. 7).

God's glory is what we should aim for, but our motives are always mixed with other concerns, especially about ourselves.

We can truthfully echo the dad in Mark 9:24 who honestly confessed to Jesus, "I believe, help my unbelief." We do not need to fear that any doubt within us or turmoil within our homes will defame God. He will be glorified regardless of our failures and weaknesses.

Satisfaction with God's Glory Advances the Refining Work He Has Begun

When we aim for and are satisfied with God getting glory in our homes, we position ourselves for his refining work. It is our own pride and our lust for respect that often get in the way of God working in our hearts. In the refining fires that we face, God will be glorified, so we can rejoice in our suffering. In these fires he brings us to humble trust and contentment with his wise and glorious purpose.

> Behold, I have refined you, but not as silver; I have tried you in the furnace of affliction. For my own sake, for my own sake, I do it, for how should my name be profaned? My glory I will not give to another.
> —Isaiah 48:10–11

In the wider context of this passage, God is explaining that he disciplines his people to refine them and to lead all things to his glory. Neither in Isaiah's day nor today do God's people's imperfections hinder the refining process or God's glory. Likewise, neither our parenting nor our teen's behavior can hinder the work of God. Nothing that eternally matters is truly at risk. God will be glorified by changes he makes in us and through us with his refining fires, "And I am sure of this, that he who began a good work *in you* will bring it to completion at the day of Jesus Christ" (Philippians 1:6).

Certainty of God's Glory Trumps Angry Intentions

The testimony of Scripture is that God will make even the wrath of man a display of his glory. The psalmist declared, "Surely the wrath of man shall praise you" (Psalm 76:10). This was clearly demonstrated in the most violent act of angry men, the crucifixion of the Son of God. Man's wrath has led to Christ being highly exalted, "so that at the name of Jesus every knee should bow, in heaven and on earth and under the earth, and every tongue confess that Jesus Christ is Lord, *to the glory of God the Father*" (Philippians 2:10–11). Believing parents can have the same assurance. God will be glorified in and through the anger and wrath that may come at them by way of an angry teen, just as he was glorified by Jesus' crucifixion.

Contentment with God's Glory Brings Comfort in Times of Distress

Paul's example in Romans 10 is valuable. Even though he knew that the Jews "have not all obeyed the gospel" (v. 16), he cited the comfort he derived from knowing that God's glory was not at risk even though he did not understand God's mysterious decree about Israel's rejection of the Messiah. These were his people. Their unbelief was a source of "great sorrow and unceasing anguish" in his heart (Romans 9:2). However, Paul found contentment in the knowledge that ultimately God would be glorified and his loving promise to save all his people would be fulfilled (see Romans 9:1–5; 22–26; 11:1–7; 25–27). "And in this way all Israel will be saved" (Romans 11:26). Paul didn't know exactly how all Israel would be saved. But he was confident that God would be glorified in every situation because everything is under his control. He concluded the passage about God's mysterious decree, painful as it may have been to him, with these remarkable words of praise:

> Oh, the depth of the riches and wisdom and knowledge of God! How *unsearchable* are his judgments and *inscrutable* his ways! For from him and through him and to him are all things. *To him be glory forever.* Amen.
>
> —Romans 11:33, 36

Even in the most baffling experiences of God's providence, believers can celebrate his glory. He is good and he will be glorified even when his judgments and ways are "unsearchable" and "inscrutable."

Pursuit of God's Glory Equips One to Persevere Through Serious Suffering

God's glory is the sole focal point believers will have in heaven after they have passed through great tribulation. It's what will matter when the saints review with 20/20 hindsight the turbulence they experienced in this life.

> After this I looked, and behold, a great multitude that no one could number, from every nation, from all tribes and peoples and languages, standing before the throne and before the Lamb, clothed in white robes, with palm branches in their hands, and crying out with a loud voice, "Salvation belongs to our God who sits on the throne, and to the Lamb!" And all the angels were standing around the throne and around the elders and the four living creatures, and they fell on their faces before the throne and worshiped God, saying, "Amen! Blessing and glory and wisdom and thanksgiving and honor and power and might be to our God forever and ever! Amen." . . . These are the ones coming out of the great tribulation . . . and God will wipe away every tear from their eyes.
>
> —Revelation 7:9–12, 14, 17

As with these saints in glory, we ought to focus on the glory of God despite (or, perhaps, because of) our anguish and tribulation in this life. Jesus affirmed that godly living will invite "tribulation" (John 16:33). Our confidence in God's power and sovereignty to bring about his glory, however, will do in us what it did for the saints in glory and for David in his stormy circumstances when Saul was pursuing him; it will produce in us a steadfast heart (see Psalm 57:7).

The benedictions in Hebrews and Jude, in the larger contexts of suffering, urge us to persevere with great hope:

Now may the God of peace who brought again from the dead our Lord Jesus, the great shepherd of the sheep, by the blood of the eternal covenant, equip you with everything good that you may do his will, working in us that which is pleasing in his sight, through Jesus Christ, *to whom be glory forever and ever.* Amen.
—Hebrews 13:20–21

. . . be glory, majesty, dominion, and authority, before all time and now and forever—Jude 24–25

Conclusion

God wants us to glorify him and enjoy him forever. His sovereignty makes certain that he will be glorified in all circumstances, even in the storms of our lives. He wants his presence and his glory to be the primary source of our contentment. Sin and anger will not dethrone him, surprise him, defeat him or embarrass him. Our crisis is "for the glory of God, so that the Son of God may be glorified through it" (John 11:4).

In the rough waters of angry teen behaviors and attitudes, before we take any action to hold our sons or daughters accountable, we need to realign our hearts and minds to care preeminently about God's glory. Other desires for our home and our teens are not necessarily wrong, but they must be put behind this one. We need to submit our wills to his. We need to remind ourselves that even in our turmoil, as a child of the light, God will indeed be glorified. His glory is not at risk. Again, hear the words of Jesus to Mary and Martha, "Did I not tell you that if you believed, you would see the glory of God?" (John 11:40). Thank him for being in control of the storm and for his victory in it and through it. Our commitment to and confidence in God's glory throughout the storm will free us to powerfully, lovingly and respectfully intervene to restore a calm sea in our hearts and our homes.

2

KEEPING YOUR FOOTING AS GOD'S PROMISES ENCOURAGE YOU

"God's solid foundation stands firm, sealed with this inscription:
The Lord knows those who are his."

— 2 Timothy 2:19 (NIV)

Some time ago, I learned that a dad of one of our high school
students was the underwater specialist who examined the wreck-
age of a collapsed pier and restaurant on the Delaware River
waterfront.

In May 2000 the restaurant Heat was full to capacity. The
music was loud and the dancing and dining were raucous. The
day before, an employee noticed some cracks at the entrance to
the restaurant on Pier 34. The next evening, people were dining
and dancing inside the restaurant and outside under a tent on the
pier that looked out over the Delaware River. Without warning
the pier collapsed into thirty feet of water.

Reports from the disaster scene described rumbling,
creaking, shuddering, volcanic shaking, a loud crash, a noise
like an explosion, and then utter chaos and mass confusion.
The floor at Heat shifted and caved in. Glass shattered. Lights

29

went out. As the pier gave way, dozens of revelers were trapped by the tent and engulfed by the river. And then suddenly, screams of terror, wild confusion. Everyone was under cold, murky water, struggling among broken planks. Metal rods, tangled wires and flotsam, alive amidst a downpour of rain at the riverfront.[1]

Several people were killed and dozens were hospitalized. The man from whom I learned of Heat's collapse into the Delaware River told me that the pilings upon which Pier 34 rested, especially at the restaurant site, had been cracked and were crumbling for years. Their support was not firm regardless of how the dancers and diners felt about their security.

The events at the Philadelphia waterfront in May 2000 illustrate well that what may *feel* like a solid foundation isn't necessarily firm. People live their lives every day on flimsy bases without any strong underpinning. They hope things will go well for them, wish for success, trust in fate, believe in a version of a god that is not at all like the biblical God, or trust lady luck or look to their lucky stars. Members of God's family, however, have a solid foundation that stands firm. The storms and threats of defiance in our homes, or any other of life troubles, can't truly harm us if we are his children. The waves may beat upon us, our earth may shake, and our mountains may be thrown into the sea, but all believers in Jesus Christ, the Rock of Ages, are secure.

Paul told young pastor Timothy that though he was suffering opposition and persecution because of his ministry, he knew that, "God's solid foundation stands firm, sealed with this inscription: The Lord knows those who are his" (2 Timothy 2:19, NIV). Our solid foundation stands firm because our Father lovingly identifies with us in Christ. The Lord knows those who are his. This knowledge is beyond knowing our names. When the Bible talks about God knowing people, it is describing God's commitment to be in a loving relationship with them. Our Father knows us. His promises are rooted in his character and are, therefore, a foundation for us to stand on that won't collapse.

God has promised to help us in times of trouble. His promises have powerful, practical effects when we face the turbulence of anger in our homes. Although we may be tempted to doubt, we can hold fast to three promises: acceptance and security in Christ regardless of our failures; wisdom when confusion or uncertainty seem to have the upper hand; and the knowledge that he will work all things, including the rough waters, for our good regardless of how they look or feel at the moment.

God promises that our acceptance and security in Christ are a solid foundation.

None of us parent perfectly. The guilt and shame that we feel when we reflect on our parenting failures can tempt us to compensate for our own sins and failures with our pragmatic strategies. We may be tempted to avoid being home where we're reminded of our failures. We may lower our demands and expectations for our kids so eruptions of anger don't remind us of our failures. We may redouble our efforts with tougher demands to get control, at any cost, in order to exclude or minimize the possibility of our failures. All of these are doomed to disappoint us and will usually compound our problems. They will not deliver the relief or success they seem to promise.

Our acceptance by our Father and our security in Christ are based on what Jesus Christ has accomplished. Our standing with God is not because of how faithful or successful we are as parents. We can't compensate or do enough to cancel out the effects of our sin and failure. Only grace is strong enough to do that. God saves sinful parents, not perfect ones. And by God's grace we have forgiveness and freedom.

> There is therefore now no condemnation for those who are in Christ Jesus. For the law of the Spirit of life has set you free in Christ Jesus from the law of sin and death.
>
> —Romans 8:1–2

It is important to remember that this promise follows on the heels of one of the most vivid passages of Scripture in which a believer battles with his own sin. The apostle Paul confesses that he does what he doesn't want to do and doesn't do the things he wants to do (see Romans 7:15–19). He concludes that "when I want to do right, evil lies close at hand" (7:21). To transport Paul's experience into a home with an angry teen is like saying, "When you talk or act like this, my own parental words of anger, impatience, overreaction, and frustration are never far from the door of my mouth. They are often ready to burst out of my heart. Sometimes they do! And I hate when that happens."

The promise that there is no condemnation for those in Christ Jesus (see 8:1) follows this confession of weakness and defeat by sin. Paul knew that believers would battle and fail and be tempted to despair or to give up altogether. So he asserts here, as he does in so many other places, that our acceptance is not because of our performance. God saves sinners who are going to continue to be sinners till they see him.

> Beloved, we are God's children now, and what we will be has not yet appeared; but we know that when he appears we shall be like him, because we shall see him as he is.
>
> —1 John 3:2

None of this excuses casualness or gives us reason to be comfortable with our sinful responses. John makes that clear when he follows up this wonderful statement of hope in the passage above with a description of the way that hope motivates us to live now. "And everyone who thus hopes in him purifies himself as he is pure" (1 John 3:3). By keeping these promises in front of our mind's eye, we will not be tempted to avoid or minimize our teen's sin or labor in our own strength to force our angry teen into compliance.

Remember, your acceptance and security are because of Christ's finished work, not yours. It is because you are "in Christ" that you have a sure, secure, firm foundation. When you give in to temptation, know that your Father invites your confession and promises to forgive your sin. "If we confess our sins, he is faithful and just to forgive us our sins and to cleanse us from all unrighteousness" (1 John 1:9). The reason he forgives is because "we have an advocate with the Father, Jesus Christ the righteous one . . . the propitiation [one who satisfies God's holy demand for justice] for our sins" (1 John 2:1–2).

Just as our sins cannot separate us from the love and acceptance of God, neither can the trials and tribulations we face in our lives. As Paul asks in Romans 8, because Christ is the one who died and God is the one who justifies, "shall anything separate us from the love of Christ?" He answers his own question with these strong words of encouragement:

> No, in all these things we are more than conquerors through him who loved us. For I am sure that neither death nor life, nor angels nor rulers, nor things present nor things to come, nor powers, nor height nor depth, nor anything else in all creation, will be able to separate us from the love of God in Christ Jesus our Lord.
> —Romans 8:37–40

Paul makes it clear that our sins and failures as Christian parents don't put our security at risk and neither do any outside threats. Our sins are forgiven in Christ. His promises are a solid foundation.

God promises that wisdom in Christ is a solid foundation.

God's general goodness works within all people to some extent and for parents it usually motivates them to look out for the welfare of their children. Theologians call this "common grace." It's his favor and kindness that are shown to the world as a whole when God causes the sun to "rise on the evil and the good" (Matthew 5:45). Likewise, his goodness is seen in the moral law of God that he's written on everyone's heart (see Romans 2:13–16). People know that stealing, lying and murder are wrong.

Godly parenting, though, does not fit into the template of common grace. That requires us to think about and apply God's Word to our lives. The Bible says that "there is a way that seems right to a man, but its end is the way to death" (Proverbs 14:12).

Parents commonly try to make parenting decisions that "seem" right to them, but "common sense" devoid of God's wisdom may *seem* right, but more often than not, "its end is the way to death." It produces more harm than good.

"Common sense" is not very sensible in God's eyes. For example, the common view is that the powerful will inherit the earth. Jesus said the meek will inherit the earth (see Matthew 5:5). The common view is that revenge is the antidote to mistreatment. Jesus said loving your enemies and turning the other cheek is the right response (see Matthew 5:39). The common view is that getting as much material wealth as possible is the way to secure our future. Jesus said giving generously to the needy is what he blesses. The common view is that an angry response to a defiant teen is justified, protects us and will win a battle. Jesus says to "bless those who curse you, pray for those who abuse you" (Luke 6:28). Common sense is not very sensible without the knowledge of and submission to God's Word. "The fear of the Lord is the beginning of wisdom" (Proverbs 9:10). Charles Bridges, in his classic commentary on Proverbs, defines the fear of the Lord as "the affectionate reverence by which a child of God bends himself, humbly and carefully, to his Father's law."[2] Submission to God's Word and seeking his wisdom is at the heart of the fear of the Lord.

God promises this kind of wisdom to parents who find themselves in confusing and difficult settings with their teen. Biblical wisdom, though, does not always give us a specific strategy to solve a problem. It is not as much related to *how* we solve a problem as it is related to *who we are* while addressing it. Biblical wisdom is more about who we are, our character, rather than what we know. Consider how James describes character-based wisdom, rather than knowledge-based wisdom.

> If any of you lacks wisdom, let him ask God, who gives generously to all without reproach, and it will be given him. But let him ask in faith, with no doubting, for the one who doubts is . . . a double-minded man, unstable in all his ways.
>
> —James 1:5–8

But the wisdom from above is first pure, then peaceable, gentle,
open to reason, full of mercy and good fruits, impartial and sincere.

—James 3:17

If one is double-minded, that is, uncommitted to being the
person God wants him to be while in a trial, he will be "unstable
in all his ways." Single-mindedness, a devotion to being the person God wants you to be, is the guarantee that you will have the
solid foundation of wise responses—even if you don't have all
the answers. Wisdom will not lead to the "ways of death;" it is
a "solid foundation" that "stands firm."

God promises that good providence in Christ is a solid foundation.

In the middle of the first century Paul wrote to the Romans to
encourage them in their faith. They were suffering greatly at the
time and would be experiencing more suffering in the decades
to come. As part of the encouragement he wrote, "that for those
who love God all things work together for good, for those who
are called according to his purpose" (Romans 8:28). This passage
is almost a cliché today. It's lost its impact for many of us because
we hear it used so casually. But it was not a casual "motto" or a
take-it-or-leave-it saying that Paul intended for the believers in
Rome. This promise assures all believers that difficult times will,
in fact, be for their good—as their Father defines good.

The reason for the soundness of this hope is because of what
the Father did in Christ. "He who did not spare his own son but
gave him up for us all, how will he not also with him graciously
give us all things?" (Romans 8:32). If our worst and most damning
enemy, our own sin, has been conquered, it is unthinkable that
God would not give us victory over the rest of life's challenges
and preserve whatever he wants to be preserved in our lives. All
other threats to us are minor in comparison to the huge threat
of sin, which he already conquered in Christ's death.

The caution we must keep in mind, however, is that we must
be submitted to the wise providence of God our Father. His

definition of things working out for "good" must be that which we seek and that for which we give thanks.

Peter speaks of God's loving promises and the solid foundation God has for suffering believers:

> Resist him [Satan and those whom he incites, such as a rebellious teenager], firm in your faith, knowing the same kinds of suffering are being experienced by your brotherhood throughout the world. And after you have suffered a little while, the God of all grace, who has called you to his eternal glory in Christ, will himself restore, confirm, strengthen, and establish you. To him be the dominion forever and ever. Amen.
>
> —1 Peter 5:9–11

Be assured, he will be glorified in your circumstances, and he will be faithful with the good he promises to you in Christ. Nothing—not the unpredictable waves of rebellion or anger from our teens or the forces of residual doubt and sin within our own hearts—can "separate us from the love of Christ" (Romans 8:39). This promise was written for believers in the real world where angry attacks against God's people occur. The Scriptures are realistic about the world in which we live and the deep water that most of us have to go through at times.

> Fear not, for I have redeemed you; I have called you by name, you are mine. When you pass through the waters, I will be with you; and through the rivers, they shall not overwhelm you; when you walk through fire you shall not be burned, and the flame shall not consume you. For I am the LORD your God, the Holy One of Israel, your Savior.
>
> —Isaiah 43:1–3

None of us are wise enough or strong enough to preserve our honor, the order and peacefulness of our homes or the future security of our children. That would be like a crippled person trying to restore his health by just willing his legs to be normal. It won't happen just because he wants it to be so. Neither do we have the power to will our family back into healthy order and ourselves into parental respectability. Believers do have one who will make their path "like the light of dawn, which shines brighter and brighter until full day" (Proverbs 4:18). They do have one who will make every ugly, painful setting work for good—as *he* defines it, which is always good and for our good. His loving promises guarantee such brightness.

Conclusion

Continuously remind yourself of your Father's loving promises to be your advocate, to give you wisdom, and to work all things together for your good. The firm footing you'll gain from focusing on his promises will help you in your rough waters. Keeping his promises in your heart will position you for the loving, respectful and firm actions you will be called to faithfully apply. It will enable you to hold your teen accountable for his self-destructive and sinful choices without being thrown off balance by his blame, excuses, rationalizations or the sheer force of his anger and threats. "Commit your way to the LORD; trust in him, and he will act. He will bring forth your righteousness as the light, and your justice as the noonday" (Psalm 37:5–6).

3

KEEPING YOUR FOOTING AS GOD'S WORD INSTRUCTS YOU

Man shall not live by bread alone, but by every word that comes from the mouth of God.

—Matthew 4:4

Your word is a lamp to my feet and a light to my path.

—Psalm 119:105

Medical misdiagnoses can be fatal.

In 2008 Tabitha Mullings, a thirty-two-year-old New York resident, was discharged from a hospital after she was diagnosed with kidney stones. She went home, and within twenty-four hours, she developed a life-threatening infection called sepsis that cut off circulation to her limbs. She was readmitted and had to have all her limbs amputated below her elbows and knees.

In January 2009, a similar error was made in Brazil. A twenty-year-old model was misdiagnosed with kidney stones and ended up having her hands and feet amputated because of a sepsis infection. She never recovered. She died a couple weeks later.

These are some extreme cases, but medical misdiagnoses can be fatal. Spiritual misdiagnoses can be fatal too. Prophets in

Jeremiah's time misled the people with faulty counsel. "From prophet to priest everyone deals falsely. They have healed the wound of my people lightly, saying, 'Peace, peace,' when there is no peace" (Jeremiah 6:13–14). Later, Jeremiah says prophets fill the people with "vain hopes" (Jeremiah 23:16).

> They say continually to those who despise the word of the LORD, "it shall be well with you"; and to everyone who stubbornly follows his own heart, they say, "No disaster shall come upon you."
> —Jeremiah 23:17

Of course Paul addresses this kind of misdirected counsel too. His words to the Galatian churches were severe. "If we or an angel from heaven should preach to you a gospel contrary to the one we preached to you, let him be accursed" (Galatians 1:8). To make sure no one moved too fast past his warning, Paul repeats himself almost exactly in the next verse.

God's Word is essential for wisdom and spiritual health. It is a sword (see Hebrews 4:12) that cuts through deception. It is a light (Psalm 119:105) that directs our path. It is the bread of life (see Matthew 4:4) that feeds and sustains us. It is a rock (see 1 Peter 2:8), that makes a firm foundation. The opening or unfolding of God's Word is useful for any situation in which we find ourselves. "The unfolding [or *entrance* in the KJV] of your words gives light; it imparts understanding to the simple" (Psalm 119:130). That is why applying it accurately and carefully is so critical. Our spiritual well-being is at stake.

The Word is a Sword for Parents of Angry Teens

Timothy lived in desperate times with out-of-control, violent, angry and defiant adults and young people in the homes of people he pastored (see 2 Timothy 3:1–5). Paul assured the young pastor that there was one resource that would equip him to help the people to whom he ministered—the God-breathed, inerrant and comprehensively useful Word of God. It is "living and active, sharper than any two-edged sword" (Hebrews 4:12). Paul said it would make the pastor who uses it "competent, equipped for every good work" (2 Timothy 3:17). Its principles extend to every situation in life.

Peter affirmed that God has given us "all things that pertain to life and godliness, through the knowledge of him who called us to his own glory and excellence" (2 Peter 1:3). The two spheres of reality that Peter identifies in this passage, earthly life and spiritual life, are thoroughly covered by God's gracious provision for his people. He has given us "*all things* that pertain to life and godliness." That provision is through "knowledge of him." The source of that knowledge is his Word. This counsel, Peter affirms, is even more dependable and certain than other special experiences we have as we'll see in the next section. It is the sharp, cutting force of the Word of God, his precious and very great promises that our Father provides for facing the "corruption that is in the world" (2 Peter 1:4). Through his Word he equips us to cut through the weeds and jungle of outside anger and pressure from our teen and directs us to untangle and settle our own inside sinful heart issues that threaten to erupt. There are no troublesome circumstances in which the Word is not relevant and effective for teaching, reproof, correction and training in righteousness (see 2 Timothy 3:16).

The Word Is a Lamp for Parents of Angry Teens

Knowing God comes from knowing God's written Word, which Peter goes on to say is the "more sure, the prophetic word, to which you will do well to pay attention as to a lamp shining in a dark place" (2 Peter 1:19). There are lots of "words" we can listen to about our own mental and spiritual health and the behavior of our teens. Those words often do not produce light. The accurate diagnosis and sound counsel from God's Word is sufficient to illumine our way. His Word shines amazing light into our homes when they seem like dark places with heavy, and sometimes overwhelming, waves of anger and confusion.

Jesus said something similar to this too. He said, "If you abide in my word, you are truly my disciples, and you will know the truth, and the truth will set you free" (John 8:31–32). Freedom rather than the heaviness and bondage that sin produces comes by practicing the truth of God's Word.

Moms or dads cannot ride out the stormy seas of angry, defiant rebellion or even aggressive indifference with the assurance that they are "doing it right" or are being truly wise if they do not follow the "sound wisdom" (Proverbs 2:7) of the Word of God. Without feeding daily on the Word, without being immersed in the principles of the Word of God, one is at best flailing wildly but blindly in deep water hoping to grab something solid to keep from drowning. More seriously, and maybe fatally, like the misdiagnoses at the start of this chapter, the problems can be compounded with the wrong prescription. Paul said that happened to the people in the Corinthian church. He said "words of eloquent wisdom" that come from the world's data banks can have the spiritual impact of making "the cross of Christ be emptied of its power" (1 Corinthians 1:17). It doesn't take much leaven to leaven a whole batch of dough. The same is true with deviant counsel that contrasts with God's wise Word.

The Word is the Bread of Life for Parents of Angry Teens

Jesus makes it clear that he, the living Word (see John 1:1 and 14), is also the "bread of life." He said "I am the bread of life; whoever comes to me shall not hunger, and whoever believes in me shall never thirst" (John 6:35). Feasting on him as the true "staff of life," the proverbial significance of bread for our bodily health, was as objectionable to his hearers as it is critical to our spiritual well-being.

People are easily attracted to the pop psychology that diagnoses problems and proposes solutions that contrast with the humbling counsel of God's Word. Just as the crowds in Jesus' day wanted a Messiah who spoke nice, respectable platitudes and did things for them (like the feeding of the five thousand in John 6), we too can be attracted to popular counsel. We tend to settle for the spiritual junk food that the world offers because it tastes better, is easier to swallow and makes us feel satisfied, even though it is slowly killing us. David described our inclination when he said, "My soul clings to the dust; give me life according to your word!" (Psalm 119:25). But our Father has spread a different table for us.

> I am the bread of life. Your fathers ate the manna in the wilderness, and they died. This is the bread that comes down from heaven, so that one may eat of it and not die. I am the living bread that came down from heaven. If anyone eats of this bread, he will live forever. And the bread that I will give for the life of the world is my flesh. The Jews then disputed among themselves, saying, "How can this man give us his flesh to eat?" So Jesus said to them, "Truly, truly, I say to you, unless you eat the flesh of the Son of Man and drink his blood, you have no life in you. Whoever feeds on my flesh and drinks my blood has eternal life, and I will raise him up on the last day. For my flesh is true food, and my blood is true drink. Whoever feeds on my flesh and drinks my blood abides in me, and I in him. . . . This is the bread that came down from heaven, not like the bread the fathers ate and died. Whoever feeds on this bread will live forever. . . . It is the Spirit who gives life; the flesh is no help at all. The words that I have spoken to you are spirit and life.
>
> —John 6:48–56, 58, 63

Jesus said that the kind of change in us that is nurtured by God comes by one's metabolizing him through his Word (see John 6:51). "Man shall not live by bread alone, but by every word that comes from the mouth of God" (Matthew 4:4). Jesus also said about the power of his word to change people: "Sanctify [*change* people into the likeness of Christ] them in the truth; your word is truth" (John 17:17). Paul says nearly the same thing when he declares, "faith comes from hearing, and hearing through the word of Christ" (Romans 10:17). Scripture never suggests that there is a magical power in just hearing the Word with one's physical ears. It always affirms that, as in the processes of metabolism of bread, we must apply and relate the Word to our situations, not just swallow it in chunks. We must break it down in order to understand its depths and to apply its truths for discernment and change. *Meditation* is the word the Psalmist uses for this thoughtful and fruitful use of God's Word.

> Blessed is the man who[se] . . . delight is in the law of the LORD, and on his law he meditates day and night. He is like a tree planted by streams of water that yields its fruit in its season, and its leaf does not wither.
>
> —Psalm 1:1–3

Your health, growth and strength, as a parent and as a Christian, are linked to your meditation on the Word of God and on Jesus. He is the true bread and staff of life. Peter uses a different spiritual nutrition metaphor:

> You have been born again, not of perishable seed but of imperishable, through the living and abiding word of God . . . Like newborn infants, long for the pure spiritual milk, that by it you may grow up into salvation.
>
> —1 Peter 1:23; 2:2

Your spiritual stamina that is needed for standing in the pounding surf of rebellion, anger and defiance from your teen will come from a nutritious diet of the Bread of Life. Feast on Him in his Word.

The Word Is a Firm Foundation for Parents of Angry Teens

No spiritual resource has been attacked more severely or consistently through the ages than the Word of God. But its wisdom for every area of life still stands intact.

Opponents directly attack the Word of God's soundness and sufficiency for every dimension of life. There is no place where such attacks are more subtle and insidious than in regard to the health of the Christian family. Attacks like these began in the Garden of Eden with Satan's effort to cast doubt on what God said to Adam and Eve. Satan provoked them to believe his lies that separated them from God and from each other. He challenged them to question God's words. "Did God actually say 'You shall not eat of any tree in the garden'?" (Genesis 3:1). When Satan incites doubt or disbelief about the validity, reliability and sufficiency of God's Word, he creates a vacuum into which his own destructive error may be squeezed. He is the thief who "comes only to steal, and kill, and destroy" (John 10:10).

God's Word is our firm foundation. Its truths are the strongest foundation we have. As the prophet Isaiah said, "The grass withers, the flower fades, but the word of our God will stand forever" (Isaiah 40:8). Jesus' parable of the two foundations in the Sermon on the Mount emphasizes the dependability of his Word to weather any storms and attacks (see Matthew 7:24–27). The storms that pound against us, whether they come from outside or inside our homes, will not prevail. Every parenting strategy other than those built on the wisdom that is in Christ and his Word will collapse and be disappointing.

Conclusion

Hearing and using the Word of God in your rough waters is not likely to be something your angry teen is about to do. But it is something you can and must do if you want the freedom that the truth produces. Much of the rest of this book will aim to unfold many of the Bible's truths for parents with an angry teen to lead to that freedom. Commit yourself to search Scripture. It's "sharper than any two-edged sword" (Hebrews 4:12). It's a "lamp" and a "light" (Psalm 119:105). Hearing and using God's Word is preeminently a heart-oriented process. Jesus said that we can't live by this world's bread alone. It is "every word that comes from the mouth of God" (Matthew 4:4) that will strengthen and sustain us. It's "living bread that came down from heaven" (John

6:51). To add yet another metaphor of Jesus: no storm, violent seas or unpredictable waves of anger or disrespect can topple anyone who stands on this rock. His Word is a solid foundation (see Matthew 7:24–27). Forever the "word is firmly fixed in the heavens" (Psalm 119:89).

4

KEEPING YOUR FOOTING AS PRAYER POSITIONS YOU

Finally, be strong in the Lord and in the strength of his might.

—Ephesians 6:10

There was a group of people in the Old Testament who wanted rest from their enemies. The prophets promised them rest in a land flowing with milk and honey. But they never got to enjoy it because they didn't trust the promise Giver.

> Therefore, while the promise of entering his rest still stands, let us fear lest any of you should seem to have failed to reach it. For good news came to us just as to them [the Israelites], but the message they heard did not benefit them, because they were not united by faith with those who listened.
>
> —Hebrews 4:1–2

The battle for minds and hearts is spiritual warfare. Like the Israelites, you must be "united by faith" to the promises of God's presence and his power for victory in your own heart and in your family. Paul made it clear that we must use all the weapons of warfare and all the spiritual armor at our disposal, including the weapon of prayer. We must be "praying at all times in the Spirit, with all prayer and supplication" (Ephesians 6:18). Prayer unites us to God for the strength and wisdom for all the resources we've addressed in these opening chapters. His strength and wisdom are necessary for us to be committed to his glory, to rely on his promises, and to receive guidance from his Word. Our victory is linked to our dependant prayers of faith:

> Some trust in chariots and some in horses, but we trust in the name of the LORD our God (Psalm 20:7).

> Not by might, nor by power, but by my Spirit, says the LORD of hosts (Zechariah 4:6)

> The prayer of a righteous person has great power as it is working. Elijah was a man with a nature like ours, and he prayed fervently that it might not rain, and for three years and six months it did not rain on the earth. Then he prayed again, and heaven gave rain, and the earth bore its fruit (James 5:16–18).

The concepts in this book are not magic. They are not quick-fix strategies that will guarantee a house free of yelling, swearing and anger in minutes or even days. This is not some five-easy-steps system to transform your teen into a model of grace and peace. Some recent TV advertisements for handling angry, defiant teens promise these changes—within a few minutes! These types of easy guarantees are like the myriad of pitches for the diet silver bullet that will allow you to eat anything you want, as much as you want and promise that you will still lose weight or develop a ripped set of abs.

The anger in our teens comes from their hearts. Our foolish responses due to our selfish desire to change our young person's behavior come from our hearts. Both our teens' hearts and our hearts must be changed. It is true that there are behavior modification strategies that can help clip behavior like the flower of a dandelion, at the surface. But these leave our teens' hearts and ours untouched. Change, therefore, is not likely to last. Similarly, because it is external only, it is not change that God will bless. Something deeper, which our earthly wisdom can't get close to, is needed.

In and of themselves the words in this book are like blanks shot from a gun. They may get your attention, scare you or your teen, and sound serious, but don't have any real power apart from the Spirit of God. Even Satan used God's words—he distorted them, of course—but Satan has no power against God's Spirit. In the end, no significant change will occur if God's words remain alone, without his Spirit in them. Such words are fired like blanks; the power of God must be in them. Pray that his Spirit will infuse all your efforts with his power to accomplish his purpose for his glory.

Plan special times for serious prayer for the Spirit's power in your own life through his Word. For the believer, praying is in order during times of serious decision-making and in the face of serious challenges. Confronting an angry teen at home fits both of those categories. Don't do it without spending time before the throne of grace calling to him in your time of need.

The writer of Hebrews gives parents guidance for serious, effectual prayer for any type of "need," including confronting the turbulence of an angry teen and the undertow temptations of their own hearts.

> For we do not have a high priest who is unable to sympathize with our weaknesses, but one who in every respect has been tempted as we are, yet without sin. Let us then with confidence draw near to the throne of grace, that we may receive mercy and find grace to help in time of need.
>
> —Hebrews 4:15–16

Three truths from these verses will help us pray Elijah-type prayers that will position us for the next serious interventions with our teen.

Recognize Your Need for a Sympathetic High Priest

Parents with angry teens don't need to be told they are imperfect parents. They know it readily enough. They may have been frustrated, exasperated, provoked, anxious, vindictive, impatient, overreactive, underreactive, resentful, distracted, hurt, despairing, unkind, abusive and angry. Sometimes they've kept some of these actions and feelings hidden under the surface, and sometimes they've allowed them to break out into the open. Sometimes they've experienced them all at once, and many times they struggle with some of them for a long time.

Parents Are Sinners Too—Like Their Angry Teen

Sometimes we take our concerns to other people in the church, in our neighborhoods, in our extended family, in the professional world. We may come away with a sense that our confidant isn't really hearing us. He doesn't really "get it."

There is a uniqueness to our personal life experiences. Solomon asserts that, "The heart knows its own bitterness and no stranger shares its joy" (Proverbs 14:10). We shouldn't be surprised that people don't understand what we are going through. Certainly there are caring folks who can gain significant levels of understanding about our trials. Similarly, there are some who can offer biblical wisdom for genuine heart-centered help. But there will always be degrees of our need or "bitterness" that no other person will be able to fully understand.

There is one, however, who *does fully understand* our heart's pain. We have a high priest who is able to sympathize with us fully. The Greek word from which we derive the word "sympathize" means to "suffer with." Jesus, the High Priest of whom the author of Hebrews is speaking, knows our weaknesses because he partook of them. His humanity was real. The pain, rejection, hatred, malignment, abuse, cursing, mockery, insults, and even physical attacks were real and experienced as real. He experienced the grief of loss ("Jesus wept," John 11:35), abandonment ("many of his disciples [not the twelve] turned back and no longer walked with him," John 6:66), betrayal ("all the disciples left him and fled," Matthew 26:56) and even rejection by his own eternal Father ("My God, My God, why have you forsaken me?" Matthew 27:46).

He understands the depths of our sin and its deadly consequences. His ability to "suffer with" us probably led to his groaning and weeping at Lazarus' tomb. He knew that he was going to resurrect Lazarus, and that the grief of Lazarus' sisters would turn to joy. But Jesus wept anyway because in his humanness he was touched by the effects of sin and its death-grip on us. The Hebrews' writer affirms this in our passage above. Jesus was "in every respect . . . tempted as we are, yet without sin" (4:15). Our High Priest sympathizes with our weaknesses.

Draw Near to the Throne of Grace

For we do not have a high priest who is unable to sympathize with our weaknesses, but one who in every respect has been tempted as we are, yet without sin. **Let us then with confidence draw near to the throne of grace,** that we may receive mercy and find grace to help in time of need.

—Hebrews 4:15–16

Jesus knows our parental weakness and our parental fallenness and has provided for them in "the blood of his cross" (Colossians 1:20). And consider the results: the writer of Hebrews tells us to "with confidence draw near to the throne of grace" (v.16).

Weak parents are invited to come with confidence (*boldly* in the KJV) into his presence with their plea for help because of Christ's effectual high priestly intercession on their behalf. We do not need to avoid calling for help because of our past record of failures with our teen or our previous neglect of prayer. God allows difficult circumstances to come into our lives to get our attention, so that we will come before his throne with our needs.

Remember the Old Testament stories in Judges. Time and again the Israelites were defeated and taken captive by their enemies. Each time God was putting his people exactly where he wanted them. He was positioning them so they would call upon him in their need and be open to his training and provision for them.

> So the LORD left those nations [the inhabitants in Caanan], not driving them out quickly, and he did not give them into the hand of Joshua. Now these are the nations that the LORD left, *to test Israel by them*, that is, all in Israel who had not experienced all the wars in Canaan. It was only in order that the generations of the people of Israel might know war, *to teach war to those who had not known it before.*
>
> —Judges 2:23–3:2 (emphasis mine)

Out of his sovereign love for his people, God places them in settings to refine and grow them for the ongoing warfare in which they will find themselves. That's what he did to the people of Israel in the land of promise. Clearly some of their own disobedience set them up for conflict, but it was not God's intent for them to face these alone, without his presence and help. The same is true for imperfect parents. Regardless of past mistakes. "Draw near to God and he will draw near to you" (James 4:8). "God opposes the proud but gives grace to the humble" (James 4:6).

Our Father delights in hearing us call to him in troublesome settings. Hebrews calls these "times of need" (4:16). Draw near to God before you proceed to the strategic sections in this book. Acknowledge your need, your weakness and your sin. Similarly acknowledge Christ's sufficient sacrifice, his open invitation, his thorough sympathy with your weaknesses as a parent. Come to the Throne of Grace with confidence. It is your Father who invites you.

Seek Mercy and Grace from Your High Priest

> For we do not have a high priest who is unable to sympathize with our weaknesses, but one who in every respect has been tempted as we are, yet without sin. Let us then with confidence draw near to the throne of grace, **that we may receive mercy and find grace to help in time of need.**
>
> —Hebrews 4:15–16

Someone has said mercy is not getting what we deserve and grace is getting what we don't deserve. When we draw near to God we "receive mercy and find grace to help in time of need" (4:16). Needy parents need mercy and grace. We've sinned in our parenting so mercy puts us in right standing with God because of Christ's death on our behalf. We are weak and face temptations so we need the provisions of grace to fight the good fight that we are in as Christian parents.

The richness of what we have in the sacrifice of Christ is opened up more fully later on in Hebrews:

> How much more will the blood of Christ, who through the eternal Spirit offered himself without blemish to God, purify our conscience from dead works to serve the living God.
>
> —Hebrews 9:14

Amazing! By his blood he purifies our consciences from our dead works. In other words the sinful efforts, sloppy obedience, inconsistent love and flagging faith that contaminate all our parenting are forgiven. There is no reason to bear guilt about any of them, even while we confess them to our Father, to our family and to our teen. Our conscience has been purified from all these dead works.

Notice also, that the reason for that purification is so that we may "serve the living God." Can this get any better! He not only purifies us, but then he commissions us to be his servants in our parent, church, neighborhood, work and every other role he gives us. Our weakness and inadequacy are not a surprise to God. That's why he, by his mercy and grace, invites us to come boldly, or with confidence, before him to find the help we need.

Our Father wants us to serve him. He has appointed us as his servants even with all our weakness. But he doesn't want weakness to characterize our ministry of parenting. He wants our weakness to be a channel for his strength to flow through. That was Paul's testimony to the Corinthians:

> So to keep me from becoming conceited because of the surpassing greatness of the revelations, a thorn was given me in the flesh,

a messenger of Satan to harass me, to keep me from becoming conceited. Three times I pleaded with the Lord about this, that it should leave me. But he said to me, "My grace is sufficient for you, for my power is made perfect in weakness." Therefore I will boast all the more gladly of my weaknesses, so that the power of Christ may rest upon me. For the sake of Christ, then, I am content with weaknesses, insults, hardships, persecutions, and calamities. For when I am weak, then I am strong.

—2 Corinthians 12:7–10

Intervene for You and Your Teen

Jesus chose twelve apostles to be with him and to be the agents for the inauguration of his kingdom work in this world. Consider the men he chose. Which didn't exhibit flaws? They all did. And finally they all betrayed him. God specializes in using weakness to accomplish his eternal purposes so that any glory that is forthcoming is his. Paul affirmed this.

God chose what is low and despised in the world, even things that are not, to bring to nothing things that are, so that no human being might boast in the presence of God.

—1 Corinthians 1:28–29

Your weakness is what God will use to bring glory to himself in your home. Allow your sense of need to drive you to call upon him for "help."

1. Plan specific times when you (and your spouse) do nothing but pray for yourselves and your need for strength, mercy and grace. Acknowledge your own inadequacies, sins, failures and temptations that show up in times of interaction with your angry teen.

2. Rest in the sufficiency of Christ for your forgiveness and the cleansing you have received in your conscience. Acknowledge your need for mercy and grace so that you may serve in the roles God has given you—especially that of a parent to an angry teen.

3. Pray for your angry teen and others in the family. Pray that God will enable you to pursue his glory first and foremost. Pray that God will be glorified in your home and through your work with your teen. Ask God to give you his wisdom, confidence in his Word and trust in his promises as you approach this mission.

PART 2

SHEPHERDING YOUR TEEN INTO DEEP WATERS

By mere words a servant is not disciplined, for though he understands, he will not respond.

—Proverbs 29:19

A few years ago, I took my family to the beach. It was like any other day at the beach. It was a hot day, the way we like it. My daughter Deb and I were out in the water. The waves were normal, and we had had a good time body surfing and diving through the waves. We went out a little farther in the water, trying to catch the right wave to get a long ride. We noticed the water was a little deeper and we had to tread water while waiting for a breaker, but before we realized it, a lifeguard was throwing a life preserver to us. We had been unaware that we were caught in a riptide and were being dragged out into even deeper water.

A riptide is a strong current that flows away from the shore into the sea. It can be gentle but strong. When a swimmer is caught in a riptide, it can be scary because he has no warning that he's being carried out to sea until he tries to swim back in to shore. The real danger is when the swimmer realizes he is being carried out to sea and tries to swim directly back to shore against the current. The effort can lead to exhaustion, which causes swimmers to drown. Alternatively, the swimmer can call for help, or if he is trained, he can escape the riptide by riding it out (riptides run in an arc and eventually flow back to the shore) or swimming perpendicular to it. To swimmers not thinking about a riptide, when it dawns on them that they are in one, their situation can be terrifying.

In our case, the lifeguard sized up our situation and got to us before any real danger occurred. He knew we were in trouble before we did. Once he threw us the preserver and we tried to swim back into shore, we began to get concerned. That's when we could feel the current because we were having to struggle against it. It occurred to us that we could have been in big trouble if the lifeguard hadn't thrown us the life preserver when he did.

In this section, you are going to learn how to allow three God-designed riptide forces to take your teen into some unexpected threatening waters. These waters will be unsettling to him because they are outside of his control. They'll take him where he doesn't want to go—in a home setting where he is responsible for the decisions he makes and must live with the consequences of them. Unlike the lifeguard who threw a life preserver to Deb and me in our riptide, we must not do the same to our angry teens. They need to sense their accountability and wake up to the fact that they are not in control of your home, its order or the life of the family.

While you are not going to throw your teen a life-preserver, you are going to shepherd him, guide or steer him, into these deep waters with your firm but compassionate care. You are not going to threaten or force your teen into these waters, issuing an ultimatum to them. However, you should gently but firmly and lovingly announce three truths to him that will make him uncomfortable and begin to sense that his position of control and power in your home is being threatened. It will begin to dawn on him that there is nothing he can do to escape these newfound deep waters. These riptide forces are out of his control.

The first riptide force to make its influence felt will be your clear communication about who you are as a parent. The second will be your acknowledgement of who your teen is as a young adult. The third will be the accountability that comes to bear on your teen in light of the first two forces.

5

THE RIPTIDE OF YOUR PARENTAL IDENTITY

Why then do you . . . honor your sons above me. . . . For those who honor me I will honor, and those who despise me shall be lightly esteemed. . . . I am about to punish his (Eli's) house forever, for the iniquity that he knew, because his sons were blaspheming God, and he did not restrain them.

—1 Samuel 2:29–30; 3:13

Tim went up to his son's room after he had slammed the rec room door and broke the window in it for the third time this year. There were battle wounds all around the house from Steven's outbursts: patched-up holes in the wall, holes that were yet to be repaired, screens that had been slashed, damaged toys and books that had been thrown and torn clothes that had been ripped in a rage. The effects from his angry temper tantrums had been getting more and more serious.

Tim hasn't always handled Steven's angry outbursts and defiance well. Sometimes Tim has gotten drawn into a verbal sparring match and ended up shouting and using some of the same vocabulary that Steven used. These encounters seemed to be occurring more frequently and ending with lots of rage from Steven and more and more threats from Tim.

Tim had been praying and seeking counsel from others in his church about how to respond to Steven's growing destructive behavior and his own reaction to Steven. His friends helped him assess his own motives and to see that they were often self-centered. He reflected on the times that he was irritable. He was often tired and didn't want to be bothered with another angry drama at home, or he was busy and didn't have time to put things aside to deal with another Steven-crisis. Tim also began to sense that some of his impatience with Steven was spilling over into his relationship with his wife—especially if they didn't see eye-to-eye in the way they should respond to Steven.

Tim humbled himself before his brothers at church and his accepting, heavenly Father. With their encouragement, Tim confessed his sins of self-reliance and unkindness to Steven and his wife to the Lord. After getting his own heart right before the Lord, he was able to be clear about his God-given parent role and then asked his wife to forgive him for his sinful insensitivity and irritability toward her. Tim discussed his plan with his wife and asked her and the brothers in his small group to pray for him as he prepared to speak to Steven. He was going to confess his failures to him and reaffirm his motives to be the parent that God had called him to be.

That evening he went up to Steven's room to talk to him.

Steven, I need to talk to you for a few minutes—not so much about you, as about me.

God has brought you into our home and made me your dad. I love you very much, though it seems I've not been real good at communicating that to you. I'm not a perfect dad. I battle with my own sinful angry responses and words to you. I haven't always listened to you as I ought to in order to understand your thoughts and feelings about things you don't like here or at school. I am truly sorry for my sins against you in all of these ways. These are not little offenses in my mind. All sin is serious. It is all destructive. Not just your sin. Mine too. Please forgive me, Steven.

But I need to share something else about my parenting that I've not always taken as seriously as I should have. It's something that I am now willing to act on because if I don't I'm sinning against you, the family and the Lord.

God has made me more than just a Christian man in your life. He's made me your father. When I stand before God, Steven, I must give account for my parental decisions or lack of them. I have asked the Lord to forgive my neglectful and weak use and trust in his Word to help me be the father that I ought to be. I know he's forgiven that. But now I must take responsibility going forward. It's never too late to begin to obey God—regardless of how we have messed up in the past.

Because God has forgiven me and has still given me the privilege and responsibility to be your parent, I am going to do that. By his grace and with his help I'm going to be the parent God has called me to be, even in ways you may not like. It is not up to me. If I'm to obey my Father, I must love you and hold you accountable for your choices—not because it feels good to me, not because I'm angry (I've done that before), not to please your mother, not to make me look good before anyone at church—because I love my Father, and he tells me that this is what love for you demands of me.

Tim did several things as he approached his conversation with Steven. First, he *humbled* himself because of his sin before the Lord. Second, he *confessed* his sin to his son. Finally, he *affirmed* his accountability to God as a parent. Tim's example follows God's pattern for all of us in a conflict situation.

Humble Yourself Because of Your Own Parenting Sins

Tim began his conversation with his son by affirming his love for Steven and then acknowledging his own weaknesses as a parent. He went on to show why his faulty parenting was serious by using David's Psalm 51 example of confession.

You are probably aware of some of your own parenting flaws and inconsistencies. You need to see your weaknesses like Tim and David saw their sins. David had murdered Uriah and committed adultery with Bathsheba, but he recognized that as bad as his sin was against these two people, primarily his sin was against his heavenly Father. "Against you, you only, have I sinned and done what is evil in your sight" (Psalm 51:4). David had to get his relationship right with the Lord before he could make amends for his sins against Uriah and Bathsheba. Likewise, Tim had to get his relationship with the Lord in order before trying to work his relationship with his son.

If you want some help in thinking through your own offenses, spend some time meditating on the lists of the common "works of the flesh" in Galatians 5:19–21 and the "fruit of the Spirit" in verses 22 and 23. It won't take most of us very long to get a sense of the scope of our offenses against our teen and the Lord. Review these behaviors and attitudes in a couple of different versions of the Bible to gain some of the nuances of meanings translators have understood the words to convey. I've copied the passage from the English Standard Version and New International Version.

> Now the works of the flesh are evident: sexual immorality, impurity, sensuality, idolatry, sorcery, enmity, strife, jealousy, fits of anger, rivalries, dissensions, divisions, envy, drunkenness, orgies, and things like these. I warn you, as I warned you before, that those who do such things will not inherit the kingdom of God. But the fruit of the Spirit is love, joy, peace, patience, kindness, goodness, faithfulness, gentleness, self-control; against such things there is no law.
>
> —Galatians 5:19–23, ESV

The acts of the sinful nature are obvious: sexual immorality, impurity and debauchery; idolatry and witchcraft; hatred, discord, jealousy, fits of rage, selfish ambition, dissensions, factions and envy; drunkenness, orgies, and the like. I warn you, as I did before, that those who live like this will not inherit the kingdom of God. But the fruit of the Spirit is love, joy, peace, patience, kindness, goodness, faithfulness, gentleness and self-control. Against such things there is no law.

—Galatians 5:19–23, NIV

Meditate on these things. Allow the Spirit of God to bring your sins to your mind. This is not something that can be done quickly. Take time to be thoughtful and prayerful. Not everything you have done as a parent has been wrong and sinful, but some of it has been. As the Holy Spirit reveals your sins to you, confess them to your Father. Don't minimize them, but identify them now as the sins that they are. Jesus said, "first take the log out of your own eye, and then you will see clearly to take the speck out of your brother's eye" (Matthew 7:5). Ask your Father to show you how any of these attitudes and behaviors have marked your relationship with your son.

The apostle John makes it clear that every believer sins (present tense) and has sinned (past tense). He says that if anyone claims to not sin or to have not sinned, he is deceived and makes God into a liar. God is not surprised by our sin. He gloriously and graciously makes provision for it by the blood of Christ.

If we say we have no sin [present tense], we deceive ourselves and the truth is not in us. . . . If we say we have not sinned [past tense], we make him a liar, and his word is not in us.

—1 John 1:8, 10

Our Father knows what we are made of. He knows we are "flesh," fallible flesh at that. Sandwiched between these two verses is our Father's welcome promise that He has made provision for his weak people. He does not leave us in despair. He assures us that we may confess our sins and find forgiveness. Our guilt and failure do not have the last word. He says: "If we confess our sins, he is faithful and just to forgive us our sins and to cleanse us from all unrighteousness" (1 John 1:9). The blood of Christ has the last word! "The blood of Jesus . . . cleanses us from all sin" (1 John 1:7).

Jesus came to save and redeem sinners, not perfect parents. He said, "I have not come to call the righteous, but sinners to repentance" (Luke 5:32). He came to empower weak parents, not strong ones. The Lord spoke to the apostle Paul, saying "My grace is sufficient for you, for my power is made perfect in weakness" (2 Corinthians 12:9). Humble yourself before your loving Father. Confess your sins thoughtfully and privately to him *before* you approach your son or daughter.

Confess Your Sins to Your Teen

Jesus said that before we will ever see clearly enough to address the speck in someone else's eye, we must first get the log out of our own (see Matthew 7:1–5). "Hypocrite" was the term Jesus used in these verses to describe someone who tried to reverse this order or would not look at his own sins at all but only at another's sins against him. You've already begun going down the right path by humbling yourself before your Father. Now you'll take that disposition into your teen's presence by confessing your offenses against him to him.

In addition to helping us see our teen more accurately—without a log blurring our vision—confession also will help us approach him or her with the humility of one sinner to another. Whether or not we intended to be speaking down to our angry teen, in the past, that is probably how he has thought about our conversations. The confession of a parent to his or her teen will not guarantee that the teen will change his opinion of us and warmly receive us, but it may turn away wrath and inhibit accusations like "you think you are better than everybody else" and "you are just a hypocrite." Most importantly, though, your confession is a step of faithfulness and obedience to the Lord.

Tim confessed his sin to his son. This let Steven know that his dad was leading from a position of weakness. This is the posture God most often chooses to use in his people. "My grace is sufficient for you, for my power is made perfect in weakness," Jesus told Paul in 2 Corinthians 12:9. The Lord Jesus is the supreme example of one embracing the weakness of humankind, "taking the form of a servant . . . being born in the likeness of men" (Philippians 2:7) to love and redeem rebellious, hateful people. He had no sin of his own, of course, but the example of Jesus' incarnation is used by Paul in this passage to direct us in our dealings with others whenever we are in a conflict. When we display this genuine attitude of humility we may see it defuse the power-play that parents and angry teens often get into when the most powerful person, the parent, comes to confront the less powerful person, the teen. The parent often tries to manipulate his teen and, like in a tug-of-war, pull him in his direction by using threats to force his authority. The teen tries to manipulate his parent and pull him his way by being loud, defiant, and threatening as well in order to get his mom or dad to leave him alone to do what he wants to do. Tim's humility helped defuse the tension. He wasn't there to threaten or demand control and force Steven to submit to him. He was there to confess his failures and affirm his love and his motives. This began the riptide effect of putting Steven into deeper water than he's been in before.

Angry teens don't have any reluctance to play the "hypocrite" card. Humbling yourself by making an accurate, thoughtful confession may not eliminate the charge of hypocrisy, but it may give your teen some hesitation before using it. Most importantly, your confession does communicate that you see your inconsistencies, sins, and failures as serious offenses against the Lord first and foremost. They are much weightier than simple offenses against your son. They are against your Heavenly Father. Steven knew that his dad saw his sins and failures as bigger than offenses against him.

In our example, Tim confessed that sometimes he had indulged Steven to keep peace at home. He'd been a weak leader at home in the way he displayed Christ's love to Steven's mother and in the way he cared for Steven's needs. Steven's forgiving response was not the important thing at this time. The confession itself was the important focus in this communication with Steven. It would be a positive move for Steven to tell his dad that he forgave him, but an angry teen may not be willing to listen to his dad with any level of openness. He may even say the opposite: "Forgive you? Are you kidding! I couldn't care less about how you feel about anything. I'll never forgive you!"

Be prepared to acknowledge your teen's rejection of your confession. Your purpose is not to wring some kind of forgiveness from your teen. It's to let him begin to get the sense that your obedience and love for your Father is what is driving you now, not your son's or anyone else's opinions. Steven is not in control—you are affirming that your heavenly Father is calling the shots now.

> I'm sorry you feel that way, Steven. But that is totally up to you. I know the Lord has forgiven me, and I just wanted you to know that I do take my past sins and failures seriously. What you do with my confession of my sins and weaknesses is entirely up to you. I'm not here to make you forgive me. I couldn't if I wanted to. This is a heart matter for you to address if you want to.

Tim was acknowledging with his confession that he is also a sinner with weaknesses. The purpose of his confession is not to initiate a certain response but to obey the Lord as a dad who wants God to be glorified in his family. Proverbs 28:13 asserts that "Whoever conceals his transgressions will not prosper, but he who confesses and forsakes them will obtain mercy." Sometimes that mercy will come from people to whom we confess our sins. However, there is no guarantee of receiving that forgiveness from them. But with the Lord, there is generous forgiveness. He does promise to forgive all who confess their sins as we saw in 1 John 1:9. It is his mercy from Proverbs 28:13 that we can count on. The spillover effects of this humble confession, as this proverb suggests, often do come from others in the family or in the church even if they don't come from our angry teen. God will be glorified in our humble obedience.

Affirm Your Accountability to God

The third thing you can do to move your teen into deeper water is to affirm that you are committed to being the parent God wants you to be. This affirmation on your part will help you do three things:

- clarify your own commitment to follow God's priorities in your parenting,
- alert the other members of your family and church to your humble but determined commitment, and
- set your teen on notice that your heavenly Father's will and glory are now your first concern in your decisions as a parent.

Your teen's threats of violence and angry outbursts, or any other manipulative strategies she has used to get her way and keep you at a distance, were going to be met with your commitment to love her by honoring your Father's wise will for you as a parent.

Tim affirmed his accountability to God as a parent when he let Steven see that he was committed to being the parent God wanted him to be in order to honor his Father first and foremost. Tim had asked the Lord for forgiveness, had alerted members of his church of his sins and commitment to change, and asked Steven for forgiveness. Now he was making it clear that he was also asking his Father to teach him how to be the father to Steven that he should be.

His Confession Clarified His Commitment to Follow God

He confessed that he had been a poor model of the godly man that Christ wanted him to be. "I must give account for my parental decisions," he said. "He wants me to take that responsibility seriously. It's never too late to begin to obey God—regardless of how we have messed up in the past."

The word *confess* is derived from a word that means "to agree." When we confess to God, we are agreeing with him about whatever he says. When I confess my sins, I'm agreeing with God that my behavior or attitudes are out of sync with his will for me. When Tim confessed his flawed parenting, he was also affirming that his commitment was now to honor God's will for his family in general and his parenting of Steven in particular.

His Confession Alerted Others To His Commitment

This kind of confession has built-in accountability measures to it. When we go public with our confessions, we open ourselves up to the encouragement, support and corrections of others. Our openness helps us stay rightly motivated to follow through on our commitment.

By letting the church and other family members know about his confession, Tim was positioning himself to be strengthened by the prayers, support and encouragement he would receive from others who cared about him and his family.

His Confession Put His Son On Notice

Tim would not be intimidated by Steven's outbursts or threats to embarrass the family or hurt his dad's feelings. His image before the church, neighbors or other family members would not be a factor in his parenting choices. His commitment was, by the grace of God, to be the man of God in his home that God wanted him to be regardless of how others would view him. He hoped Steven would recognize this single-mindedness on his part, but his parenting would not be determined by whether he did or didn't take his dad's commitment seriously.

Conclusion

All three of these truths—humbling yourself, confessing your sins and affirming your God-appointed parent identity—like a riptide, will begin to drag your teen to a place in his mind that he has not visited for a while—the uncomfortable place of uncertainty about his status. He may begin to get a sense that something is changing and that this might affect him. You are beginning to take away some of the excuses your teen has used to keep the focus of blame on you for his attitudes and behaviors instead of looking seriously at himself.

You're not defending your sinful reactions. You've just confessed them. You're not excusing your mixed motives in your parenting. You've exposed them. You've recommitted yourself first and foremost to please and honor God in your parenting and no one else. You have recognized your parental identity in Christ, including the authority that has been given you over your family that he delegated to you. In doing so you explain that you are accountable to God and have laid the foundation for letting your teen know that you will be holding him accountable for his actions and attitudes—because God says to do so.

This is just the beginning of the riptide current of understanding that your teen will begin to sense. The second feature of this current to dawn on your angry teen will be the different way you now acknowledge his identity.

6

THE RIPTIDE OF YOUR TEEN'S IDENTITY

I have perceived among the youths, a young man lacking sense
. . . he does not know that it will cost him his life.

—Proverbs 7:7, 23

After Tim humbled himself, confessed sins and failures as a parent and affirmed his own God-appointed parent identity, he was ready to talk to Steven about his God-appointed young adult identity. Steven was a teenager, and in biblical terms, teens are young adults. This was going to add to Steven's inner conflict. He wanted to be treated like an adult and yet, when he began to sense where this conversation could lead, he thought that maybe he didn't want to be treated like an adult, after all. Tim continued his talk to his son:

> Steven, one of the mistakes I've made in my relationship
> with you has been to treat you like a child. You are not a child.
> You are a young man, and I've been really slow to see that.
> The Bible identifies young people your age as young men,
> not children. It recognizes that you have all the basic abilities

that I have as an older adult. That's why the book of Proverbs addresses young people and older folks alike with topics like money, listening to correction, sex, hard work and laziness, planning for the future, how to choose friends, how not to be seduced by women, anger, self-control and much more.

Another similarity you and I have is that we are both accountable to follow God's wisdom about life. When we ignore or violate his wise counsel, we will usually have to live with the consequences of doing so. As a young adult you have more freedom to make decisions about your life than when you were a child. When you were younger, if you chose to lie, your mom or I would discipline you and that pain was usually enough to make you think twice about lying again. As an adult, though, the stakes are higher. If you choose to lie, you teach people to not trust you, and they limit how much freedom or restriction to give you. Lying can have a serious effect on your young adult options. Likewise, if you break the speed limit or drink alcohol underage, other authorities come into play, and the consequences can be even more life-limiting. You could get into an accident, injure someone or someone's property, suffer serious financial loss, lose your driving privileges or even go to jail.

Parents try to prevent their young children from making serious, life-threatening mistakes by limiting the freedoms that they have to the maturity they are showing. When they do cross lines that they shouldn't, wise parents bring painful consequences their way so they make the connection between their choices and outcomes that follow.

We're both recognized as adults, in biblical terms, Steven— you a young adult, because you are still under my authority— and me a full adult. This doesn't make me any better or any smarter a person than you. But it is God's way of describing us to help us recognize the authorities we are under. I'm under the authority of my boss, the pastors of the church, the police and other officials appointed by the government. You are under these folks too *and* under my authority as your parent. I've not always thought about this as seriously as I should have, Steven. But because I am committed to being the parent God wants me to be, I'm planning to take your accountability and my own more seriously.

Tim stressed two important biblical themes when he talked about his son's identity: 1) that teens are young adults and not children and 2) that choices have consequences.

Teens Are Young Adults

The most common word used in the Old Testament for young people between puberty and age thirty is *na'ar*. It is translated in the Old Testament "youth" or "young man"—or some similar term for this age range of young people—about 250 times. Even today in Jewish culture, boys and girls at age thirteen are recognized to be young men and young women in the bar mitzvah and bat mitzvah ceremonies.

We see the na'ar identity of teens mentioned in several familiar Bible stories. In Genesis 37:2, Joseph was seventeen and was identified as a na'ar, or "boy." In Daniel 1, Daniel and his three friends were called na'ar, or "youths," when taken under the king's care for training (see Daniel 1:4-5). David, the youngest boy in the family, was called a na'ar, or "youth," by Goliath (see 1 Samuel 17:42). Solomon identifies the young adults we usually call teenagers in Proverbs 1:4 when he wrote that wise counsel is "to give prudence to the simple, knowledge and discretion to the youth (na'ar)."

The verses from Proverbs 7, under the title of this chapter, speak of the na'ar's accountability in sexually seductive situations and the severe, life-threatening consequences to crossing the lines of morality. Most Hebrew scholars have understood Proverbs 7 to be about sexual immorality but others see the sexual temptation in this chapter as a metaphor for all forms of idolatry to which a young person may be tempted. In all of the cases listed, however, the Hebrew term is referring to someone who is more than a child and who has adult capabilities, responsibilities and accountability, and experiences consequences connected to his decisions.

In his conversation with Steven, Tim began by affirming his identity as a young adult. He acknowledged that he didn't always take that seriously in his parenting but that he was planning on doing so now. He was going to respect Steven's young man identity. He was one whom God had brought to a point in his life in which his decisions were *his* decisions and the positive benefits or the negative consequences of his choices would follow *his* choices.

Tim summarized some topics in Proverbs to show Steven the range of freedom and responsibility that he had. Read or skim Proverbs 10–29 to get an idea about the adult themes Solomon covers in this book of wisdom. The counsel in these areas is for adults both young and old to heed. They include choice of friends, responsibility for getting wisdom, matters relating to money, immorality and prostitution, generosity, the poor, the rich, speech, listening, responses to correction, work and laziness, decision-making, crisis planning and much more.

These are topics for older and younger adults. Na'ar have all the capabilities of full adults, all the accountability of full adults, but not all the freedom. That is why they are identified as *young* adults.

Young Adult Choices Have Consequences

Steven may have felt a sense of victory when he thought, "Finally, Dad realized I'm not a little kid anymore." But that may have been short-lived. Steven squirmed a bit on the inside as he became more aware of this feature of young adulthood. Steven liked the idea of being treated like an adult. Most teens do. Angry teens really do—if that means getting the freedom they want. What they often don't like is the connection of that freedom with their responsibility for their choices. This conversation took Steven into deeper water than he was comfortable being in. Of course, that's the point.

Tim helped Steven link his adult identity to choices he might face. Lying as a young adult teaches people whether or not to trust him. This can limit his options and freedoms if the people he's lied to are authorities to whom he must answer. Driving over the speed limit could play out in dangerous ways too. He could lose his license or, worse, get in a bad accident. Drinking underage invites a whole host of consequences, including the possibility of going to jail. Tim's illustrations were signaling both Steven's accountability and his dad's willingness to respect that young adult status. Tim wanted his son to know that while he had not been as faithful and wise a father in the past, his intention was to show that respect to him now. He was going to allow Steven's choices to determine the freedom he could enjoy as a young adult.

While parents cannot *make* their sons or daughters honor and obey them, and the Lord, they must insist upon obedience and respect, and try to make these responses by their teen more appealing than defiance or disobedience. Young adults are their own persons with their own wills, motives and commitments. But parents must hold them accountable for their choices. In the next chapter and all of part three, I offer biblical guidance for holding your teen accountable. There is a non-negotiable link that God makes between being a young adult and being accountable. Parents need to be abundantly clear about this connection because their faithfulness and love may require their costly obedience to allow serious consequences to come into their teen's life because of their irresponsibility or defiance.

The Old Testament high priest Eli and his sons are tragic illustrations of the costs of not making that link. "The sons of Eli were worthless men (na'ar). They did not know the LORD" (1 Samuel 2:12). Eli was rebuked by the Lord for not holding his two sons responsible for their shameful immoral and irreverent behavior as people brought sacrifices to the tabernacle. When people brought offerings for sacrifices, Hophni and Phinehas would not follow the Levitical guidelines for sacrificing but found ways to force

people to give them the best cuts of meat and fat, which were to
be burned as part of God's offering. Just as shameful, they were
having sex with the young women who were serving with them at
the tabernacle. Eli knew about this law-breaking and did nothing
but to mildly rebuke them:

> Now Eli was very old, and he kept hearing all that his sons were
> doing to all Israel, and how they lay with the women who were
> serving at the entrance to the tent of meeting. And he said to them,
> "Why do you do such things? For I hear of your evil dealings from
> all the people. No, my sons, it is no good report that I hear the
> people of the LORD spreading abroad. If someone sins against a
> man, God will mediate for him, but if someone sins against the
> LORD, who can intercede for him?" But they would not listen
> to the voice of their father, for it was the will of the LORD to
> put them to death.
>
> —1 Samuel 2:22–25

God sent a prophet to Eli to rebuke him for his weak-willed,
concerned-for-what-others-think parenting. He challenged Eli
about his destructive priorities.

> Why then do you scorn my sacrifices and my offerings that I com-
> manded, and honor your sons above me by fattening yourselves on
> the choicest parts of every offering of my people Israel? . . . those
> who honor me I will honor, and those who despise me shall be
> lightly esteemed.
>
> —1 Samuel 2:29–30

A few verses later God relates his message of judgment on the
house of Eli to the young apprentice Samuel:

> And I declare to him [Eli] that I am about to punish his house
> forever, for the iniquity that he knew, because his sons were blas-
> pheming God, and he did not restrain them.
>
> —1 Samuel 3:13

The tragic story of Eli and his sons illustrates several principles that show how serious it is for parents to hold their young adult children accountable.

First, we need to fear God over man. In Proverbs 29:25 we see that the fear of man is a trap. We fear God over man when we care more seriously about either what God says or what others expect about our behavior and priorities. Eli's rebuke of his sons was more like apologetic pleading. "It is no good report that I hear the people of the LORD speaking abroad" (1 Samuel 2:24). His concern for the report he hears from others seems to be more important to Eli than his concern for the LORD's revealed "report" in his Word. God's Word about the sanctity of priestly work was clear. Eli's neglect was a way of honoring his sons more than honoring the LORD. Whether he was afraid of his sons or afraid of what other people thought of him, we don't know. Perhaps it was both. But it is obvious that Eli was more concerned about his own interests than God's honor.

There is a right concern we ought to have for the perspectives and opinions of others. We want others to gain a right view of God, his Word and of the richness of a relationship to Christ when they look at our personal lives and our home life. But our desire for others to have a good opinion of us must never trump our obedience to how God's Word directs us to live and parent our children. Eli allowed the way others saw him and his family to be of greater concern than obedience to God's law about worship and righteous living.

Part of Tim's failure may have been to have some of the same fears that Eli had. What Tim was sure of now, though, was that because he loved Steven and his Heavenly Father, he was not going to honor his son or fear others more than the Lord's clear parenting directives. He was going to respect Steven and his choices by holding him accountable for them. Tim was careful to let Steven know that he was not going to be manipulated by what other people thought of him. He was going to parent as God wanted him to parent. He was going to love and respect his teen as God directed and trust God for the outcome.

In the past Tim would have been shaken by Steven's angry condemnation, "All my friends' parents think your rules are crazy and unreasonable. My friends can't stand coming here." These are hurtful things to hear. Yet, Tim was determined, by the grace of God and with the feedback from other trusted brothers and sisters, to honor the Lord more than his son or his son's friends and his son's friends' parents.

Second, parents need to hold unbelievers and believers accountable. Eli's sons were unbelievers. Their spiritual state, however, did not excuse Eli from holding them accountable for mocking God and their parents. Proverbs 30:11 asserts with gruesome frankness, "the eye that mocks a father and scorns to obey a mother will be picked out by the ravens of the valley and eaten by vultures." God condemns attitudes of disrespect and the behaviors of contempt for a parent's authority in anyone in whom they are found.

God's moral law applies to everyone—whether they profess faith in Christ or not. In Ephesians 6:4 Paul writes, "Fathers, do not provoke your children to anger, but bring them up in the discipline and instruction of the Lord." He does not say that parents are commanded to bring up only their believing children in the discipline and instruction of the Lord. Scripture affirms that disrespect and contempt for parental authority must be addressed. It's a serious matter that if left unaddressed will have destructive consequences—often in this life, but always in eternity.

The wise writer of Proverbs observed, "Do not withhold discipline from a child; if you strike him with a rod, he will not die. If you strike him with the rod, you will save his soul from Sheol" (Proverbs 23:13–14). Somehow the outside is connected to the inside. God has designed painful consequences to follow foolish decisions in most of life—for older adults and young adults. There are exceptions in our broken world as Psalm 73 and the entire book of Ecclesiastes illustrate. But in God's eternal design of things, "If you are wise, your wisdom will reward you; if you are a mocker, you alone will suffer" (Proverbs 9:12, NIV).

Third, parents must not minimize sin. Eli's neglect was not that he didn't talk to his sons. It was that he didn't take firm action to restrain them or remove them from office. Even if Eli knew ahead of time that God's secret purpose was to put his sons to death for their blasphemous and immoral behavior that would not excuse him from holding his sons accountable. Deuteronomy 29:29 directs us to practice what we know and not to be paralyzed by what we don't know, or by what others think they know. "The secret things belong to the LORD our God, but the things that are revealed belong to us and to our children forever, that we may do all the words of the law." It is revealed truth that sets people free (see John 8:32).

Proverbs 29:19 says, "By mere words a servant is not disciplined, for though he understands, he will not respond." Some people under authority are unwilling to submit to that authority. Defiant teens are like this. They have their own ideas, values and wills, and they are not going to heed your legitimate directives and expectations no matter what you *say*.

It is right, of course, for parents to explain what is expected of their teen and what boundaries are wise and required in their home. No amount of explanation, however, will rein in a defiant young adult. Mere words won't persuade him. Action is needed. The implication is that parents need to allow "painful" consequences to take their toll on a defiant young adult. Illustrations about a variety of "painful" options will follow in the next chapters. Eli was unwilling to inconvenience himself, "make a scene" and do the hard things necessary to honor God more than his sons. When he should have taken action to stop his sons' sinful behavior in the temple by relieving them of their duties, instead, all he did was plead with them with words.

Tim was putting Steven on notice, subtly and gently. He explained that *more than words* were going to be forthcoming since words, to that point, were not getting through.

Fourth, we need to embrace suffering for ourselves and allow it for our teen because it produces humility and grace. As we hope God will use suffering in the life of our young adult to mature him,

God also uses suffering to mature us as believing parents. Unless we see that the suffering we will experience in godly parenting is God's good plan for us as well as our teen, we will back away from it or, at least, dull its sharp edges by half-hearted or weak actions or talk as Eli did. Knowing God's rich pathway for us is through suffering will embolden us to be faithful and loving to our angry teen—even while our hearts are torn apart and our tears are mocked.

James tells us to

> Count it all joy, my brothers, when you meet trials of various kinds, for you know that the testing of your faith produces steadfastness. And let steadfastness have its full effect, that you may be perfect and complete, lacking in nothing.
>
> —James 1:2–4

Maturity, completeness, growth comes through the hardness of trials. Paul asserts the same thing in Romans and Philippians:

> For I consider that the sufferings of this present time are not worth comparing with the glory that is to be revealed to us.
>
> —Romans 8:18

In the next verses from Romans 8, Paul finally concludes that such suffering and groaning ultimately is for our good. "And we know that for those who love God, all things work together for good" (v. 28).

In Philippians, Paul actually connects suffering in the believer's life with his calling to faith. "For it has been granted to you that for the sake of Christ you should not only believe in him, but also suffer for his sake" (1:29).

Both our faith and our suffering are labeled as a "calling" in this passage. In our parent roles we will suffer—especially if we seek to be faithful in the area of bringing accountable pains into the lives of our angry teens. Our hearts will break. We will grieve and fear for their futures. Our relationship with our teen will be threatened—maybe for all of life. In terms of our pride, our suffering will call into question (a needed and very good thing) our status as good parents, respectable neighbors, model church members, Bible teachers, youth workers, counselors, pastors, etc. Yet such suffering will be used by our Good Shepherd to conform us to Christ, mature us in the faith and focus our heart passion to be content with knowing him more and more deeply. That's how Paul said suffering was used by God in his life:

> Indeed, I count everything as loss because of the surpassing worth of knowing Christ Jesus my Lord. For his sake I have suffered the loss of all things and count them as rubbish, in order that I may gain Christ and be found in him, not having a righteousness of my own that comes from the law, but that which comes through faith in Christ, the righteousness from God that depends on faith—that I may know him and the power of his resurrection, and may share his sufferings, becoming like him in his death, that by any means possible I may attain the resurrection from the dead. Not that I have already obtained this or am already perfect, but I press on to make it my own, because Christ Jesus has made me his own. Brothers, I do not consider that I have made it my own. But one thing I do: forgetting what lies behind and straining forward to what lies ahead, I press on toward the goal for the prize of the upward call of God in Christ Jesus.
>
> —Philippians 3:8–14

The Apostle Peter also teaches that suffering is an invaluable tool of God to bring about our personal defeat of sin in our lives:

> Since therefore Christ suffered in the flesh, arm yourselves with the same way of thinking, for whoever has suffered in the flesh has ceased from sin, so as to live the rest of the time in the flesh no longer for human passions but for the will of God.
>
> —1 Peter 4:1–2

Any area of life in which one overcomes something, masters something or becomes skillful in something pain and suffering are involved. The same is true for us as we bring up our children in the discipline of the Lord (see Ephesians 6:4).

We live in a culture that is myopic and misdirected. It tells us that most, if not all, suffering is bad. We must not allow our parenting to be numbed or paralyzed by cultural "wisdom." God's Word is clear. We must hold our teens accountable. The suffering for them and for us that will come as a consequence of our loving actions will be used for good as God has stated—regardless of how it feels at the moment.

In our modern world, Tim could be intimidated by the popular culture's preoccupation with Steven's need for a high self-esteem, to feel good about himself, or for his need to express himself and not have his spirit crushed by rules and restrictions. The ethic of fun and pleasure has become the touchstone for how worthwhile something may be in western culture. American values consider suffering a great evil. It cannot be good for people to suffer—especially young people. After all, they haven't lived long enough to do that much harm to others to deserve suffering. Young people need to have fun. They need to be free to enjoy life.

Like Tim, you must not shy away from pain and suffering that comes with your parental accountability and from holding your teen accountable. Avoid the Eli-syndrome of fearfulness or complacency. While we don't like to see any loved one suffer, parents with defiant teens should be thankful for any measure of suffering their teen experiences. God's school for growth, maturity and even spiritual sensitivity is often the school of pain, loss and suffering. Suffering may come from outside sources (police, lawyers, principals, doctors, bankers) or from our parental obligation to bring respectful, loving discipline into our young adult's life. We'll address the significance of suffering for parents in the hostile world today at the end of Part Three.

Needless to say, Steven may be thinking to himself, "I want to be treated like an adult, but I'm not sure what you are saying about accountability and pain." His idea of being treated like an adult is probably to be left alone to do what he wants to do when he wants to do it—without any interference from anybody. He is not going to be thrilled at the direction in which his father is taking him. This isn't what he had in mind when he thought of being treated like an adult. It's clearly not what his dad has had in mind in the past. These riptide forces are taking Steven into deeper threatening waters.

7

THE RIPTIDE OF ACCOUNTABILITY

If you are wise, your wisdom will reward you; if you are a mocker, you alone will suffer.

—Proverbs 9:12 (NIV)

William Jefferson Clinton, the President of the United States, didn't understand why Congress was trying to impeach him. He had apologized for his sexual indiscretions and acknowledged them publicly. Shouldn't that settle the matter? He believed that his apology should have ended any further concern with his personal failures. He thought if he apologized and the people forgave him then there should be no consequences.

Repentance, however, is a process of restoration in which forgiveness is just one part. If the offense is minor, such as using a harsh word with someone, an apology is all that may be required. If the offense is egregious, such as an assault on someone, an apology is just the beginning. There may also be other more serious consequences.

Our angry, defiant teens (and much of the Western culture) hold to Bill Clinton's concept of forgiveness. Asking for forgiveness should cancel out any further punitive or disciplinary consequences. Steven had the same opinion about forgiveness. Steven was getting a sense of where his dad was going with the talk about his parental identity and Steven's identity as a young adult. The riptide of these truths was beginning to carry him along to a new awareness. "Somehow or other," he thought, "there is going to be some unpleasant twist and turn of consequences in the way mom and dad will be dealing with me." It may be at this point that he fires the Bill Clinton "forgiveness" or "apology" salvo.

Dad, I'm really sorry for taking the ten dollars off the table and swearing at you guys when you tried to get it back. I let my temper get the better of me. I know you have been meeting with those guys at church and are on this accountability kick. So I'm sorry. And didn't Jesus let the woman caught in adultery go when her accusers didn't stone her? (John 8:7–11). I said I was sorry. Doesn't being a Christian mean that you should forgive me? Jesus said to forgive people seventy times seven (Matthew 18:22), didn't he? What more do you want? I said I was sorry and it won't happen again!

Your teen may not be as savvy about quoting the Bible as Steven thought he was. (John 8 is not about parenting but about the Scribes' and Pharisees' motives to trick Jesus and condemn him. And Matthew 18 is not about forgiving without consequences but about the unlimited nature of forgiveness.) But segments of this collection of arguments often do emerge in one way or another, and we need to be ready to answer them with truth. Jesus forgave the woman, but she still was punished with shame and humiliation. Even though we are called to forgive an unlimited number of times, Proverbs 13:24 tells us that "whoever spares the rod (a literal and metaphorical source of pain) hates his son, but he who loves him is diligent to discipline him."

In the ongoing conversation between our teenagers and us, there are three truths that we must share with our teens at one time or another: biblical discipline is positive, it's a process and it's painful. These truths will help us answer our teen's false ideas about forgiveness or the significance of an apology. They may not accept our explanations. In fact, the defiant, angry teen who accepts these truths about sin and consequences readily is predictably rare. According to Proverbs, "a scoffer does not listen to rebuke" (13:1). If they are true to form, they'll insist that you are not being fair or making sense. They'll say that you are being stupid and hateful. "And," they'll charge, "you call yourselves Christians?!" Hold fast. We must be clear, in our own minds, that painful consequences must follow angry, disrespectful behavior, especially where forgiveness has been granted. God's forgiveness of us was not without consequences. The punishment was taken by his Son in our place with all the horror and agony included in hell, separated from his Father. But there were painful consequences just the same.

Three Truths about Biblical Discipline

One of the most significant New Testament passages from which to draw principles for parental discipline is Hebrews 12. It describes how our Heavenly Father deals with us.

Consider him who endured from sinners such hostility against himself, so that you may not grow weary or fainthearted. In your struggle against sin you have not yet resisted to the point of shedding your blood. And have you forgotten the exhortation that addresses you as sons?

> "My son, do not regard lightly the discipline of the Lord, nor be weary when reproved by him. For the Lord disciplines the one he loves and chastises every son whom he receives."
> It is for discipline that you have to endure. God is treating you as sons. For what son is there whom his father does not discipline? If you are left without discipline, in which all have participated, then you are illegitimate children and not sons. Besides this, we have had earthly fathers who disciplined us and we respected them. Shall we not much more be subject to the Father of spirits and live? For they disciplined us for a short time as it seemed best

to them, but he disciplines us for our good, that we may share his holiness. For the moment all discipline seems painful rather than pleasant, but later it yields the peaceful fruit of righteousness to those who have been trained by it.

—Hebrews 12:5–11

This passage summarizes the way the Father relates to all his children. It is a model for all parents. This pattern of discipline is especially helpful to parents with a rebellious teen because any of us in these trying times can lose sight of the positive nature of discipline, the extensive process of raising godly children, and the valuable role that pain plays in the life of our teens. It is appropriate to view this passage as a pattern for us to follow because the writer of Hebrews brings earthly parenting into this picture as a comparison for our understanding.

From this passage, there are at least three immediately useful principles that will affect your interaction with an angry, defiant teen. Biblical discipline is positive, biblical discipline is a process, and biblical discipline is painful. Parents must be clear about all three if they are to respectfully hold their teen accountable.

Biblical Discipline Is Positive

The object of biblical discipline is training. It is not punitive justice like the death penalty. It is the corrective love of a parent for his son or daughter. Our Father's intervention is proof of his love for us. It is also his instrument to produce the "peaceful fruit of righteousness to those who have been trained by it" (Hebrews 12:11).

In the wisdom literature, the word *instruction* is closely connected with discipline. The ESV translates Proverbs 1:2 to show the purpose of the book "To know wisdom and *instruction.*" The Hebrew word *musar*, here translated as "instruction," is commonly used by Solomon and the other sages of Proverbs. It is also translated "discipline." "Whoever spares his rod, hates his son, but whoever loves him is careful to discipline [musar] him" (Proverbs 13:24). When our children are young it is our job to discipline them so that when they are older and out from under our authority they will remain disciplined in their own lives. To not discipline them and train them would be the same as hating them in Solomon's view. He says this because their lack of discipline will set them up for their own self-destructiveness, selfishness and arrogant treatment of others who don't give them what they want when they want it.

Old Testament scholar Bruce Waltke points out that instruction (musar) "is connected with discipline and rebuke; it is learned this way and by keen observation and cogent reflection on the suffering of others."[3] We will discuss this in more detail in the third truth, but his point is that training, education in general and discipline are inseparable. Teaching our children about telling the truth and disciplining them when they don't, for example, helps them lay a foundation for the future of every sound relationship they will ever have. Trust is critical with friends, employers, teachers, neighbors, your own children and our walk with the Lord. If there is no truth-telling or only partial truth-telling, there will at best be only partial trust, lots of doubt, suspicion and shallowness in a relationship. Disciplining lying is instruction about wise living in Solomon's view. Other verses in Proverbs 13 use the same Hebrew term but ESV scholars translate it as "instruction."

A wise son hears his father's *instruction* [musar], but a scoffer does not listen to rebuke (Proverbs 13:1).

> Poverty and disgrace come to him who ignores *instruction* [musar], but whoever heeds reproof is honored.
>
> —Proverbs 13:18

The message of the sages of the Old Testament, and that of the apostles, is that parents are to train their children. Training our children cultivates the qualities of character that align with wisdom. It includes pain, as we'll see later, but its goal is to encourage young people to make the connection between their *wise* choices and the reward that flows from them (Proverbs 9:12). This fruit doesn't grow naturally. That's why discipline is not a once-and-done event, but a process.

Biblical Discipline Is a Process

Like Steven, our teens may have scores of objectionable behaviors that need to be changed. We'd like to see our teen handle disappointment without rage. We'd like them to obey us without an argument and speak respectfully when we ask them or tell them to do something. We'd like them to consider others in their decisions more readily than their own interests and be generous instead of demanding. We'd like them to be truthful and above reproach instead of carrying a cloud of suspicion about most of what they say or do. We'd like them to be respectful of other people's property, treat siblings with care and respect and eliminate cursing and profanity from their vocabulary. The list goes on. We want to see these things in our teens because they are evidence of maturity, and, most important, they are signs of righteousness. But, in the same way that our Father disciplines us little by little, moving us one step at a time closer to the character he wants to be formed in us, we need to pace our expectations for our teen's changes. Like our Father's dealings with us, we need to be patient and choose a few things at a time to work on.

> Beloved, we are God's children now, and what we will be has not yet appeared; but we know that when he appears we shall be like him, because we shall see him as he is. And every one who thus hopes in him purifies himself as he is pure.
>
> —1 John 3:2–3

Jesus followed this same pattern in his training of the twelve disciples. He said, "I still have many things to say to you, but you cannot bear them now" (John 16:12). He knew that the disciples could only handle so much at one time, just like us, and just like our teens. As we saw earlier in Hebrews 12:1–5, we "struggle against sin" (v.4) and we are not to be "weary when reproved by him" (v.5). In other words, God doesn't expect all the changes to be made at once. Instead he urges believers to "run with endurance . . . looking to Jesus . . . who endured the cross, despising the shame" (vv. 1–2). That transformation is a process. What we will be is not yet what we are, and only when we see him will our fullness be complete.

This delay in our own sanctification, or our Christlikeness, doesn't justify complacency on our parts. Our Father's will for us is to "be holy . . . as he who called you is holy" (1 Peter 1:15, 16). Total Christlikeness is what God is producing in us—over time and into eternity. The pain we endure by standing up to opposition or persecution along with life's hardships and the pain involved in the spiritual warfare with our hearts, the world and the devil are all part of his wise plan. When we pace our expectations of our teen's changes and focus our discipline on a few sins at a time, we're not excusing other features of their rebellious behavior. We're just recognizing that change is usually a gradual process in their lives just like it is in our own lives. We are nurturing our teen's respectful behavior with discipline and accountability one stage at a time.

Biblical Discipline Is Painful

Training and instruction are what parents are commissioned to bring into the lives of their children. Old Testament scholar Bruce Waltke observes in his exposition of Proverbs that, "in Egypt, the word for 'to rear' is accompanied with a determinative of a man holding a rod."[4]

> Whoever spares the rod hates his son, but he who loves him is diligent to discipline [musar] him.
>
> —Proverbs 13:24

Such training includes the pain of discipline. The New Testament continues with this same line of parenting counsel:

> Fathers, do not provoke your children to anger, but bring them up in the *discipline and instruction* of the Lord.
>
> —Ephesians 6:4

Steven could tell that his dad was approaching him differently. In the past Tim threatened to take things away from Steven if he would not change his behavior. More often than not, however, Tim and his wife backed away from the threats they made because they were made out of anger and were extreme. They'd tell him, "If you argue with us about this curfew again, you'll go to your room and not come out for a week!" or, "If you speak like that again, you will be grounded for the next three months!"

Sometimes they wouldn't follow through with their threats because they didn't know how to enforce them. "I know we said that if we got another bad report from school he'd lose all Internet privileges, but how can we do that? He needs the computer for his classes. And besides, we're not always home to monitor his computer use."

Sometimes Steven's mom and dad didn't carry out their threats because they were intimidated. Steven's rages became louder and more violent whenever they threatened to punish him. Instead of addressing the issue biblically, they tried to keep the peace by accommodating his angry outbursts. They would leave the room or tell him to go to his room when he got angry, thus all the holes in his wall. Their house was like a minefield or road laced with hidden IEDs (improvised explosive devices). Tim and his wife never knew what would trigger his rage. No one was comfortable being there.

After Tim's conversation with Steven, he sensed something was different. His dad was not going to be accommodating anymore. It sounded like he was going to follow through with consequences that he'd invited by his behavior.

Some time ago a boy was visiting the zoo and saw a keeper go into the cage with a large lion pacing around its one end. The boy watched the keeper drop some meat in a pan and sweep up some of the lion's waste. He turned his back on the lion a couple of times in the process of doing his job. The boy was almost shaking with fear for the keeper.

When the keeper came out of the cage the little boy asked, "Sir, weren't you afraid of being attacked by the lion?"

"Nah," the keeper replied casually. "Nothin' to be afraid of. He doesn't have any teeth."

When we don't follow through with our threats of discipline when our children are young, we train them to behave as though mom and dad don't really mean what they say. The lion of discipline has no teeth. When they get older our teens will be bold as well if they sense the lion of discipline has no teeth.

> By mere words a servant is not disciplined, for though he understands, he will not respond.
>
> —Proverbs 29:19

The example mentioned earlier of Eli and his lack of discipline of his two sons illustrates the serious effects of such benign warnings and commands. (It also illustrates God's abhorrence of this kind of parenting.) His sons were put to death because Eli honored his sons more than God by allowing them to persist in their wickedness rather than holding them accountable.

Following through with our discipline as parents means more than just talking to them. It means we need to hold them accountable with a form of punishment that will be uncomfortable or painful to them. Jesus uses the picture of a gardener pruning "every branch that does bear fruit . . . that it may bear more fruit" (John 15:2). For younger children such pruning (or punishment) can include a variety of things like spankings, time-outs, standing in a corner, or going to bed without dinner. For older kids it may need to be more creative, such as not having screen time (with TV, computer games, etc.), losing access to their texting privileges, their phone, being in earlier, not getting a driver's permit, etc. The important thing, though, is that the lion of discipline needs to have teeth; the discipline needs to hurt.

Pain is not the opposite of love. Hatred is. Yet, our culture often insists that anything painful must be evil. Every achieving athlete, student, musician, artist, contractor or part of a job training program knows that some level of pain and self-denial is critical to become good or skillful. Doing what comes naturally will leave us mediocre at best and destructive at worst. Consider a complacent, self-centered athlete's impact on a team, for example. Our Father's wise choice of painful discipline of his children is perfectly measured, rightly timed and lovingly administered to yield the peaceful fruit of righteousness (see Hebrews 12:11) in all of his children. Our choices of painful discipline for our teens must follow our Father's example.

Perfectly Measured

Wisely applied discipline must be measured carefully to fit the offense. Forgetting to take out the trash is not the same as a daughter sassing her mom or using profanity because she is not getting her way. Correction is important in both cases, but the sting should not be as painful for some offenses as it is for others. Paul asserted that parents should not "provoke your children to anger" (Ephesians 6:4) "lest they become discouraged" (Colossians 3:21). He's *not* saying, "Never do anything that crosses the will of your child or over which they become angry or discouraged." Discipline that is painful, like our Father's, is going to elicit some kind of reaction—teen anger or discouragement may be forthcoming from good and godly well-measured parent discipline.

Paul is teaching parents to use measured methods and approaches that are thoughtfully and lovingly applied. How a teen reacts will be dependent upon what is in his heart. Jesus said, murder, slander, foolishness, "all these evil things come from within" (see Mark 7:20–23). Even teens in the Old Testament times who reacted violently and with disrespect were to be stoned to death by the community. Their parents didn't *cause* their reactions. Our discipline should be measured out carefully to not be unnecessarily provocative of anger or discouragement but neither should it be neglected or minimized for fear of angry responses.

Our Father like our Savior does not quench smoking flax or break bruised reeds. But neither does he deal with kid gloves when firm discipline is required. In the book of 1 Corinthians, Paul makes reference to the discipline that some in the church were experiencing because of abuses of the Lord's church and the sacrament of Lord's Supper. "That is why many of you are weak and ill, and some have died" (11:30), he said. In Proverbs 30:17, Agur describes in a dramatic and violent way the judgment of God against one with a dishonoring attitude toward the parents God has appointed in his life: "The eye that mocks a father and scorns to obey a mother will be picked out by the ravens of the valley and eaten by the vultures."

Rightly Timed

Solomon affirms that "For everything there is a season" (Ecclesiastes 3:1). In Proverbs, Solomon applied the principle of timing to daily interactions among neighbors as well as to words of correction.

Whoever blesses his neighbor with a loud voice, rising early in the morning, will be counted as cursing (Proverbs 27:14).

A word fitly spoken is like apples of gold in settings of silver (Proverbs 25:11).

In both cases, Solomon's wise counsel is to consider the setting and timing of your communication. If these words of wisdom are to be generally applied in our normal conversations with neighbors, they are even more applicable when talking to an angry teen.

The best time to talk to an angry teen is usually not in the heat of the moment. Timing is important. The goal is not to get things "off your chest." The goal is a godly response on your part to bring about a helpful conversation that may include learning and change on the part of your teen. You must do everything you can on your part to be controlled by your Father's agenda of bringing about loving accountability.

The tongue of the wise commends knowledge, but the mouths of fools pour out folly (Proverbs 15:2).

A gentle tongue is a tree of life, but perverseness breaks the spirit (Proverbs 15:4).

Select a time to talk when you or your teen is not rushed, not angry, not hungry and not anxious about something else. Let the storm of anger or anxiousness pass before you try to get into the boat and make headway.

Sometimes the most powerful thing a parent can do is admit she doesn't have all the answers and needs time to think about a response. Most of the time there is no reason to have to declare an emergency and take immediate action when the sirens are blaring and the lights are flashing and the noise of explosions is in the air. Godliness is your goal. Not having the last word at that moment.

Lovingly Administered

Our Heavenly Father disciplines his children in an atmosphere of love and acceptance. Godly parents follow his example. Neither of these qualities makes us close our eyes to or make excuses for disrespect or defiance. But they often do smooth the way for better communication. Love and painful discipline are not, as our culture believes, opposites. "For the Lord disciplines the one he loves, and chastises every son whom he receives" (Hebrews 12:6).

An angry teen, though, will not likely interpret your loving and accepting spirit in a favorable light. In fact, she will often accuse you of exactly the opposite. "You don't love me," is a manipulative strategy that has worked for her in the past or one that she's seen other teens use with their parents. Your love and acceptance, however, don't need be acknowledged by your son or daughter to be genuine. Your tone and manner must dominate your demeanor even when you are affirming the most unacceptable things to your teen.

Part of Tim's conversation with Steven showed both of these effects.

Tim: Steven, I'm not angry with you and I'm not trying to threaten you. But I need to follow up on some of the earlier conversation we had. Satan uses people's anger as a way of taking them captive to do his will. Jesus tells us Satan's aim is always to kill, steal and destroy. I do have some very strong things to say to you, but we believe that God has put you in our family by his good plan, Steven. We love you and can't just overlook what will hurt you or others in our family.

Steven: I don't care what you say! You don't know what love is. Your spiritual stuff is hypocritical. You just want me to fit into your mould, and I'm not going to do it. I don't want to be here, and I'm leaving as soon as I can.

Tim: Does it look like I'm angry with you, Steven? I'm not. I don't like some of the things you've been doing and saying; they have often been hurtful. But they don't make me love you less or even make me angry with you. My deep concern is that this spirit I see in you is going to destroy you and hurt others you love and who love you.

It may not be easy to see Tim's spirit by reading his dialogue, but what he says comes from a right spirit and a thoughtful heart. He is not idealistic or unrealistic as he expresses his love and concern to Steven. He acknowledges Steven's uncooperativeness or hurtful words and actions in a loving way and then opens the door to discuss the hard requirements that he is going to implement in his home and demand of Steven out of his love for him.

Love does not avoid inflicting pain on a loved one. The pain of discipline, rebuke or correction is called a "wound" in Proverbs. These wounds can be faithful offerings of love to a friend or a son. "Faithful are the wounds of a friend; profuse are the kisses of an enemy" (Proverbs 27:6). "Kisses," or as the cliché in our culture expresses the idea, "kissing up to someone," can be manipulative and deceitful. Such sweet, "soft and fuzzy" words may seem loving, but "hatred" is how God describes the real disposition of one who does not bring painful "wounds" into his son's life when they are warranted. "Whoever spares the rod *hates* his son, but whoever loves him is diligent to discipline him"

(Proverbs 13:24, emphasis mine). *Hatred* is not too strong a word for someone who would allow his child to develop patterns of sinful behaviors or attitudes that will lead to trouble in this life (see Proverbs 9:12) and suffering in eternity:

> Do not withhold discipline from a child; if you strike him with a rod he will not die. If you strike him with the rod, you will save his soul from Sheol [the grave].
>
> —Proverbs 23:13–14

A parent may "feel" sentimentally loving toward his son by not allowing him to hurt from the consequences of his actions. His son may even cheer his mom or dad on before others as someone who understands him and trusts him (lets him off the hook). Love without disciplinary care, however, is emotional sentiment that some have called "dumb love." This "love" will bear ugly fruit. It is crippling love that will result in a young person's bondage to his temper when things don't go his way.

Loving administration of discipline means that you must be in full, Spirit-controlled self-control. This may mean you need to take time for your own heart to be settled and to see clearly, think clearly, and plan wisely how to talk to your teen. The heat of the moment is not usually conducive to loving confrontations.

Conclusion

One important caution: These principles of accountability and discipline won't change your teen's heart. Even the most loving and accepting discipline does not substitute for the work of the Holy Spirit. Your prayer for the work of God in your young adult should accompany your faithful, careful application of the biblical principles sketched throughout this book. If we lose sight of this need to appeal to God throughout all our conversations and actions with our teen, we do no better than the moralist or behavior modification psycho-therapist. Ultimately, significant and lasting heart change will only occur when our young adults embrace Jesus as their Savior and King. Pray that every time you apply these principles, each moment of contact and each conversation, you will display the power and richness of Christ to your young adult and that the Holy Spirit will use your love and words to break his heart and yield repentance and faith. The history of the church gives abundant testimony that God can conquer angry, defiant people. The life of the apostle Paul illustrates God's power to change angry people. He was one "breathing threats and murder" to believers (Acts 9:1) but God turned him around. He can do that with any angry, determined young adult, too.

Riptides carry us to places we don't plan to go. Adopting our parental identity and accepting our teen's biblical identity, and bringing biblical measures of accountability lovingly into our teen's life can be used by the Holy Spirit to take your teen where he is reluctant to go. With the work of the Holy Spirit, God may use your faithfulness in this parent pilgrimage to also give repentance and faith to your young adult. Most of all, however, your faithfulness will help you to honor the Lord in your parenting with a difficult teen. In the next part, we'll explore specific ways to apply these disciplinary principles to your defiant teen by respectfully, yet firmly, holding him accountable.

PART 3

ALLOWING YOUR TEEN TO SINK IN DEEP WATERS

(Sinking is not drowning)

For you cast me into the deep, into the heart of the seas, and the flood surrounded me . . . my life was fainting away, I remembered the LORD, and my prayer came to you, into your holy temple. . . . Salvation belongs to the Lord.

—Jonah 2:3, 7, 9

There are two accounts in Scriptures where God used deep waters to teach a lesson. Both Jonah and Peter were allowed by their all-wise Father to sink in deep, rough seas.

Jonah sank because of his waywardness and rebellion. God told him to go to Nineveh and preach repentance. Instead, Jonah boarded a ship going in the opposite direction. When the sailors found out the storm was because of Jonah's disobedience to God, they threw him into the sea. The LORD sent a great fish to swallow him whole. It was while in the depths of the sea that Jonah confessed and submitted to the will of the Father (see Jonah chapters 1–2).

Peter sank because he took his eyes off Jesus. One night the twelve disciples were in a small boat on the Sea of Galilee. They were in the midst of a storm when the Lord came walking on the water to the disciples. They were terrified. They thought they saw a ghost. Jesus called to them to calm their fears, and Peter, in his zeal and at the Lord's invitation, got out of the boat and walked toward Jesus. He sank when he took his eyes off of Christ and put them on the threats of the storm around him. He was more focused on his situation than on his Lord (see Matthew 14:28–30).

God used these deep-water experiences to strengthen Peter and Jonah's confidence in his loving plan and deepen their immediate submission to his wise purpose. These experiences did not mark the last time Jonah and Peter needed to be rebuked and put back on the right path of obedience. Jonah sulked in anger after God showed mercy to Nineveh (see Jonah 4), and Peter ignorantly rebuked the Lord (see Matthew 16:22) and later denied him three times (see Matthew 26:69–74). These deep-water experiences were not "silver bullets" in either of their lives. God took both of them into deep-water experiences, however, to grow further in their faith and faithfulness. He let them sink, feel the fear and anxiety of sinking and left them there until they called for help.

Some, like Peter, may call out for help quickly. Others, like Jonah, may need to go down to the roots of the mountains where the weeds wrap about their head and the waters close in over them (see Jonah 2:5–6). As our teens spend time in the deep water produced by their willfulness with its murkiness, coldness and weeds, God may use their condition to create the alarm and desperation that Jonah and Peter felt to nudge them toward repentance.

There are three truths to clarify with your teen that will cause him to sink in deep and muddy waters and to feel the threats that come with his own folly: teens have privileges, not rights; privileges only come with responsible choices; privileges only come with respectful attitudes. We must allow deep-water experiences to engulf our disobedient, angry and defiant teen. If our young adult is humbled by the sensation of sinking, God will graciously restore him as he did with both Jonah and Peter. God extended this offer to Israel, his chronically wayward people, when they were threatened with the very deep water of captivity.

> Therefore I will judge you, O house of Israel, every one according to his ways, declares the Lord GOD. Repent and turn from all your transgressions, lest iniquity be your ruin. Cast away from you all the transgressions that you have committed, and make yourselves a new heart and a new spirit! Why will you die, O house of Israel? For I have no pleasure in the death of anyone, declares the Lord GOD; so turn, and live.
>
> —Ezekiel 18:30–32

Sadly, they refused God's gracious invitation at the point of his offer. But later many did turn to him in humility and repentance. That is our prayer for our teen—that sooner, rather than later, he'll turn back to the God of goodness and love in Christ.

In this section we will learn ways to let our teen sink in over their head and then how to help them get their footing once again—if and when, by the grace of God, they want it.

8

MAKE THE WATER DEEP

BY DIFFERENTIATING
PRIVILEGES AND RIGHTS

God is not mocked, for whatever one sows, that will he also reap.
—Galatians 6:7

Teens have no rights! This was the foundational principle that the authors of *Toughlove,*[5] a parenting strategy devised by psychologists David and Phyllis York to help parents bring order to their homes and love their rebellious teens. Their discoveries grew out of their own pilgrimage with their two defiant teens. After seeking family therapy from several professionals, they grew weary of having their teens sit in sessions and get off the hook for their behavior while they were blamed over and over again by therapists for provoking their teens' rebellion. If only they would get their act together as parents their teens would be acting right. It was their fault their teens acted out.

Many of the principles of *Toughlove* sound like the wisdom in Proverbs, though they did not intentionally write their book from a biblical perspective. But the York's first principle is also a fundamental assumption in the wisdom of Proverbs—written about three thousand years earlier. They were not saying that teens should not be loved, respected or raised responsibly. They were asserting that the *things and opportunities* that teens come to expect and take for granted as their "rights" are not rights at all. They are privileges. They agree with the wisdom of Proverbs on this point.

God Does Not Give Us Our "Rights"

There is no verse in Proverbs that specifically says "teens have no rights!" But the underlying principle permeates Scripture and is especially evident in the hundreds of connections the wisdom literature makes between behaviors and attitudes and their outcomes. Clearly, the testimony of Scripture is that the only "right" any of us has is to be judged as guilty of breaking God's law and to be deserving of his judgment. "All have sinned and fall short of the glory of God" (Romans 3:23). Paul also asserts that the "wages of sin is death" (Romans 6:23). For those who trust Jesus Christ as their Lord and Savior, of course, God interrupts that eternal death destiny. He gives them eternal life "if you confess with your mouth that Jesus is Lord and believe in your heart that God raised him from the dead, you will be saved" (Romans 10:9). Jesus himself described this eternal life interruption of our death destiny in the common gospel summary in John 3:16: "For God so loved the world, that he gave his only Son, that whoever believes in him should not perish but have eternal life." A perishing destiny is the normal trajectory for us all. God in his mercy and grace interrupts that otherwise certain future and provides the only way for us to avoid getting what we deserve, our right of judgment.

God Gives Us Privileges Out of His Goodness

However, while we and our teens have no rights, God's common grace, his generally displayed goodness to all people, usually does allow us to enjoy the benefits that he links to living in harmony with his good and wise will for righteous behavior. Ultimately, God makes life work this way in order to position people to seek him (see Romans 2:4 and Acts 17:24–27). As noted earlier, however, people don't always experience God's goodness the same way. We live in a broken world, are broken ourselves and live with other broken people. Sometimes the sinfulness of mankind and the brokenness of the sin-infested world breaks on people who do appear to be doing well. Generally, though, God makes it possible for undeserving, angry, inconsistent, unfaithful people—including parents like this writer and the readers of this book, and their young adult children—to enjoy the benefits that flow from his goodness. This usually happens when our behaviors and attitudes line up with the wise counsel of his Word, whether we are conscious of it or not. I've noted this verse earlier, but it's worth repeating:

> If you are wise, your wisdom will reward you.
> —Proverbs 9:12, NIV

There is a serious connection between righteous living and beneficial life experiences. Old Testament scholar Derek Kidner notes that this verse is one of the clearest statements in Scripture about the connection between personal choices, accountability and outcomes.[6] Another Old Testament scholar, Bruce Waltke, says this verse "underscores the doctrine of individualism,"[7] meaning that each person is the ultimate reaper of positive or negative consequences by his wise or foolish choices. The New Testament testimony of this connection between choices and outcomes is clear too. "Do not be deceived," Paul says. "God is not mocked, for whatever one sows, that will he also reap. For the one who sows to his own flesh will from the flesh reap corruption, but the one who sows to the Spirit will from the Spirit reap eternal life" (Galatians 6:7–8). Paul says that God links life outcomes to our moral and spiritual choices. This is clear from the immediate context that delineates the works of the flesh, the fruit of the Spirit (see Galatians 5:19–23) and positive or negative consequences that flow from the lifestyle choices one makes.

Privileges Can Be Lost Because of Idolatry

When our teens confuse privileges and rights, they are vulnerable to the bankruptcy of idolatry. Idols can only do one thing:

make promises with words that entice us. The irony, of course, is that we are the ones who put words into an idol's "mouth." Then we live our life according to the agenda it sets for us, and we experience loss in many ways because we are living according to our idol's empty promises.

For example, the angry teen who believes he should be able "to do what I want to do when I want to do it and answer to no one," is blinded by the idol of a false notion of "freedom." Paradoxically, this "freedom" only enslaves him and doesn't give him freedom at all. Three thousand years ago, Solomon illustrated this:

> One who wanders from the way of good sense will rest in the assembly of the dead. Whoever loves pleasure will be a poor man; he who loves wine and oil will not be rich.
>
> —Proverbs 21:16–17

Verse 16 illustrates the paradox of the young person who doesn't practice good sense (God's wise counsel about living) in his choices because they don't seem very appealing. He wanders or lives thoughtlessly doing what he wants to do when he wants to do it. He ends up with nothing but irretrievable loss in the assembly of the dead. Solomon illustrates this more specifically in verse 17 with someone who doesn't merely use pleasure for refreshment as God intends it, but someone who is dominated by it as a consuming lifestyle. His pleasure-oriented life led him into patterns of self-indulgence that led to poverty. Idols always lie, deceive, mislead and bankrupt their worshipers.

Privileges Can be Lost by an Angry Teen

Consider the angry teen mentioned above. He demands his own way or his own preferences in his own time. Is such a teen free to move on to the next level of academic or professional preparation in school? No, because he only studies what he wants to study when he wants to study it. Is such a teen free to get any job he wants to get? No, because no employer wants someone who only wants to do his own will his own way. Is such a teen free to have lots of friends and close relationships? No, because dependable friends look for people who care about them and not only themselves. The point is that all idols lie. These lies come from the father of lies, the devil, and he only comes to "steal and kill and destroy" (John 10:10). Listening to the appeals of idols ultimately leads to moral and spiritual bankruptcy. A kind of life-paralysis.

The psalmist illustrates this graphically. Speaking of the nations around Israel, the psalmist describes the foolishness and absurdity of living life with loyalty to any god but the true and living God.

> Their idols are silver and gold,
> the work of human hands.
> They have mouths, but do not speak;
> eyes, but do not see.
> They have ears, but do not hear;
> noses, but do not smell.
> They have hands, but do not feel;
> feet, but do not walk;
> and they do not make a sound in their throat.
> Those who make them become like them;
> so do all who trust in them.
> —Psalm 115:4–8

Notice the net effect of this idolatry: "Those who make them become like them." The paralysis of idols illustrates the net effect of idolatry in our lives. If we organize our lives around the agenda of the popular idols of our world, we can expect to be just as immobile, unproductive, dependant, impotent and "stupid" (a strong word but one used by God as in Proverbs 12:1) as they are.

Teens want freedom. But the very thing they passionately crave will be out of their reach without wise parents who allow their young adults to experience losses of privileges that will flow from their allegiance to the idols in their hearts.

Loss of Privileges in the Old and New Testaments

The Old Testament prophets illustrate the futility of trusting anything other than God. He alone is God. Idols are nothing and can deliver nothing. Some passages come close to actually mocking idol worshipers.

> When you cry out, let your selection of idols deliver you! The wind will carry them off. A breath will take them away.
>
> —Isaiah 57:13

> All who fashion idols are nothing and the things they delight in do not profit. . . .

> They know not, nor do they discern, for he has shut their eyes, so that they cannot see and their hearts so that they cannot understand. No one considers nor is there knowledge or discernment to say, "Half of it I burned in the fire; I also baked bread on its coals; I roasted meat and have eaten. And shall I make the rest of it an abomination? Shall I fall down before a block of wood? He feeds on ashes; a deluded heart has led him astray, and he cannot deliver himself or say, "Is there not a lie in my right hand?"
>
> —Isaiah 44:9, 18–20

Idolatry is absurd! But it is alluring to us in so many subtle ways. It promises shortcuts to prosperity, success, power, attention, pleasure, future security, health, happiness, purposefulness and meaning, and every other value that is attractive to us. Notice the last verse from this passage. These people can't even bring themselves to admit that their idol is of their own making—that it is "a lie in my right hand." It has totally captivated them.

In Matthew 4 Satan tries to entice Jesus with a range of temptations that he also waves in front of us to lure us away from the first two great commandments, to love God and our neighbor. Satan tried to attract Jesus with the idols of comfort, control and approval. If he would turn the stone to bread, he would satisfy his hunger. If he would worship him, Satan would give him all the world's kingdoms. If he would jump off the pinnacle of the temple and show the Father's spectacular deliverance, he would receive acclaim and fame by everyone. But idolatry always leads to loss to one degree or another in believers and unbelievers. It did tragically for us all in Eden but not in Gethsemane. "Therefore, just as sin came into the world through one man, and death through sin, and so death spread to all men because all sinned" (Romans 5:12). But the Savior responded with righteousness and did not capitulate to the deceiver's lies and snares. Comfort, approval and control appeal to our young adults just as strongly as they do to all adults. Loss is the outcome of listening to the messages these idols announce.

Consider Israel's history. Did God ever remove the privileges of the Promised Land from his errant people? How about the privileges of health, freedom, abundance, security and authority? Even the barest familiarity with the stories of the Old and New Testaments will yield examples of God doing just that. The stories of Cain and Abel, Jacob and Esau, Moses and the rock, Israel's forty years in the wilderness, Israel's captivity in Babylon for seventy years, the deaths of Ananias and Sapphira, sickness and death in the Corinthian church and John Mark's defection from the apostles' first missionary trip all illustrate the loss that comes with self-centered, idol-infested living.

Their heart affections for other gods provoked the true, living God to drive Cain from the community and mark him because of his murder of Abel. He cursed Jacob with familial strife and gave him sons who imitated his dishonesty and deceitfulness. He forbade Moses to enter the Promised Land because in his anger he struck the rock with his staff against God's instructions. He made Israel wander in the wilderness for forty years because they wouldn't trust him in the face of their Canaanite enemies. He used unbelieving Babylonian leaders to discipline his idolatrous and unrighteous people and to remove them from the land of promise to Babylon. He took the lives of Ananias and Sapphira for lying to the church about their so-called, generous giving. He disciplined some in the church of Corinth with loss of health and life because they did not take church worship seriously. He discredited John Mark for a time, in Paul's and the church's eyes, because he abandoned their first missionary journey.

Anger, jealousy, willfulness, strife, covetousness, favoritism, deceit, fearfulness, flippancy, betrayal and other destructive practices all flowed from living with an agenda other than God's. He offers "every good gift and every perfect gift" (James 1:17). Their choices led to the painful loss of the privileges of enjoying God's goodness.

Tim's Ongoing Conversation with Steven

Tim was in Steven's room. He just finished affirming his intention to respect Steven as a young man with real choices of his own. But before he can go on to talk about Steven's accountability he needs to clarify the difference between "rights" and privileges.

I love you very much, Steven. You don't see that right now, and I accept that. I can't control that. One of the things God tells me that I am accountable to do for you is to help you understand that privileges are privileges and not rights. God's Word teaches that there is an important link between our choices and the privileges we get to enjoy. This is the way he treated people throughout all of history. You know some of the stories. Adam and Eve enjoyed the privilege of the garden but their disobedience led to their exclusion from it. The people of Noah's day enjoyed their prosperity and the culture was thriving, but God judged them with a flood because they abused them. Moses enjoyed the favored leadership of God's people but later forfeited the privilege of entering the land of promise because he didn't obey God's directive. David experienced uncommon prominence as a godly leader, but his immorality led directly to the death of his baby and, later, to the rebellion of his son Absalom, who himself lost his life through his defiance. There are many more examples of people losing their privileges because they'd chosen to live following the beat of a different drummer than God. All these people enjoyed the advantages of living under the authority of God, but they lost the privileges of peace and prosperity when they took them for granted and turned their backs on Him. They came to think that they deserved these good things. They believed that they had a right to the blessings of God regardless of their behaviors and attitudes toward the Author and Source of them.

These same standards are the way God, my Father, deals with us, Steven. We're no different than Adam and Noah and David. And I'm no different than you. The privileges I enjoy— owning a car, owning a home, having a family, having a job, being able to relax at times—are gifts from God and are linked to my willingness to make wise choices. You've heard the verses, "whatever one sows, that will he also reap" (Galatians 6:7), and, "If you are wise, your wisdom will reward you; if you are a mocker, you alone will suffer" (Proverbs 9:12, NIV).

Soon Tim is going to assert that he is not going to be taking things from Steven as punishment. Steven is waiting with bated breath to hear his dad's threats to do this. He is ready with his own counter-threats and angry words. That is the way the conversation has gone before. But Tim is *not* going down that road this time. Tim is affirming that Steven's privileges are his privileges to enjoy as he makes the choices for responsible, respectable young adulthood. Instead of Tim taking things from Steven, Steven is deciding whether to enjoy the advantages of his privileges or not to enjoy them by his own choices—as did the people in the Old Testament he mentioned. This is very important in the process of helping Steven make a connection between his behavior and the privileges that go with it. This is also critical because it removes Tim from the role of confronter, policeman, dictator and despot.

Clearly Tim will ultimately have the parenting responsibility to enforce Steven's decisions to enjoy or forfeit privileges that are at his disposal. But keeping this clear in one's mind as a parent is important to help Steven make the connection between his behaviors and enjoying the things he likes. Until Steven begins to get the message, he will probably respond with his typically angry retorts, accusing his dad of being unfair, unreasonable and taking things from him. But Tim must continue to sing this chorus, "I'm not taking things away from you. You are choosing to not enjoy them. They are privileges for you to enjoy by behaving responsibly or to lose through wrong choices. You know the kind of choices you can make any time to be able to have full use of the privileges that are open to you."

This is not just a matter of semantics. It's not just verbal trickery, slick salesmanship or manipulation. It's a subtle difference but it makes a real difference—in mom's and dad's thinking and, when it finally clicks with Steven, in his thinking. Steven has learned in the past that if he messes up, in the words of his dad or mom, he loses things or they try to take things from him. They are the bad guys, taking his stuff from him. Now that charge is going to be seriously undermined. His privileges will be connected to his choices—he's in control.

This will be addressed more completely in the chapters ahead. Right here Tim is especially trying to emphasize that privileges come with a price-tag, and that they are privileges, not rights.

> You have many things that you've become used to enjoying, Steven. But you don't have a "right" to them. They are privileges. Your room, the car, your iPod, your cell phone, your computer, the money you earn or that is given to you—these things may be yours, but you don't have a right to use them any way and at any time you choose. They are privileges that your mom and I want you to have and enjoy but not at the expense of hurtful, disrespectful and dishonoring attitudes, words and behaviors. These things are privileges that come with responsible, respectful and honoring attitudes, words and behaviors.
>
> We can't make you behave honorably and use respectful speech toward us. God has not given us some magical power

to force you to make good choices. But we do have the responsibility to try to help you make the connection between your choice of attitudes, words and behaviors and the privileges that you'd like to enjoy.

Conclusion

The first truth that will send your teen into deep water is that he has no rights, only privileges. In this conversation you'll affirm that you are obligated by God to respect your son. This means you'll allow him to enjoy the privileges and opportunities according to the choices that he makes to respect the people God has placed in his life. Don't insist that your teen respond well to your presentation. He may or may not. You can't control that. Ask the Holy Spirit to enable you to see the big picture of your Father's call on you as a Christian parent. Don't allow your teen's response to intimidate or distract you from your goal to lovingly and faithfully parent.

9

MAKE THE WATER DEEPER

BY ATTACHING PRIVILEGES TO RESPECTFUL AND RESPONSIBLE CHOICES

For the moment all discipline seems painful rather than pleasant, but later it yields the peaceful fruit of righteousness to those who have been trained by it.

—Hebrews 12:11

In the last chapter we saw that our teen has no rights. It is by the grace of God that we have the opportunity to enjoy any of God's goodness at all. Here we'll expand on how our choices, our behavior and attitudes, affect our privileges. Tim *began* to show Steven that there is a link between his choices and the privileges he enjoys. In this chapter we'll focus more specifically on that linkage with responsible choices. God makes this connection with his children for their benefit and for his glory, and we must make it with ours. Responsible, biblically wise choices yield enjoyment. At the same time, unrighteousness is the way to forfeit the pleasure of the privileges he makes possible for us.

This next step will help you to shepherd your teen into deeper water by respecting his choices of behavior and connecting them to the privileges he wants to enjoy.

Privileges Come from Good Choices

Tim was not primarily "taking things away" from Steven. That's the way he's usually approached disciplinary measures with Steven in the past. Now he would be saying that the privileges were going to be attached to right behavior and attitudes. Notice the contrast of approaches with this mother and her teenage son:

Her former approach

- "If you don't clean up your room by dinner time, you will miss it for the night."
- "If I get reports from your teachers that you are not turning in your work on time, you will be grounded on the weekends."
- "If you don't use respectful language in our house, you will lose your phone and computer privileges for the week."

Taking things away from someone is an act of power. It is one person's challenge to another person's freedom to do what he wants to do when he wants to do it. It is confrontational. Angry or defiant teens are familiar with power plays with authority figures—you, the teachers, administrators at school, church people, the police, etc. The teen doesn't necessarily win but the relationship between them and the adult authority is typically only strained by the confrontation. At best an adult can wring a behavioral change out of the teen but not out of any sense of personal responsibility—just out of fear of you, the power broker and your possible punishment.

On the other hand, giving your teen the power to choose whether he will be able to enjoy a privilege is a diffusing alternative approach. Consider some important assumptions that the mother is using in each of the conversations below. (We'll explore them a little later.) The question to be considered here is, who decides whether or not the teen has access to the privileges at his disposal?

Her current approach

- "Tom, we want you to eat with us tonight, but you know that getting dinner depends on whether you've fulfilled your responsibility to have your room cleaned by 6:00 p.m. If it's not, you know what decision you've made, right?"

- "Tom, you have some great plans for the weekend. We want you to be able to enjoy them, but you know we need email confirmation from your teachers that you've turned in all your work for you to enjoy that privilege."

- "Tom, you are welcome to use the phone with your friends if you choose to use language that is respectful and honorable toward us throughout the week."

Which approach is likely to increase the heat and tension in the relationship and which may more likely reduce it? Which is likely to be rejected as a power play or a threat and which approach puts the ball in the teen's hands? Putting these expectations in positive terms gives us another way to make the point of how privileges are connected to good choices and impress upon your angry, defiant teen that the choice is up to him.

In Proverbs, there are hundreds of connections between our wise choices and the blessings and privileges in which we delight. There are also hundreds of connections between our foolish choices and pain and suffering—more than three hundred of each, by my count. The wise parent in Proverbs recognizes that the one who determines the blessing or curse (in terms of human responsibility) is the young adult himself. It's not that dad and mom are arbitrary, despotic or authoritarian monarchs. (Although, that is how an angry and defiant teen probably sees it.) Instead, parents are clearly agents in the disciplinary process. They must remind their teen that their actions—the blessings and the curses, the gains and the losses, the freedoms and the restrictions—are in response to his choices.

Our parental goal is not to "win" an argument and "score points." We want to see heart change in our teen to the glory of God. This means we want to communicate as effectively as possible. My previous book, *Get Outta My Face!*, addresses communication with angry teens at length. Proverbs has much godly counsel for us in this matter. A few of the verses that are applicable here are:

> "The tongue of the wise commends knowledge, but the mouths of fools pour out folly" (15:2). Solomon is urging careful, thoughtful attention, *before* you speak to people in order to make information palatable, attractive, and desirable.

In contrast to this, "A fool takes no pleasure in understanding, but only in expressing his opinion" (18:2). When you have an agenda to promote you are not interested in understanding another person's perspectives or thoughts or disposition. They are irrelevant.

> "The heart of the wise makes his speech judicious and adds persuasiveness to his lips" (16:23). When you are interested in persuading someone about something, you will think carefully about your choice of words, their timing and the way they will be heard. You will tailor your speech to communicate a godly message to the best of your ability in order to persuade.

Tim said Steven's responsible choices would be connected to his freedom to enjoy his privileges and implied that his foolish choices would forfeit them. Tim diffused what would have been a confrontation with Steven by putting the responsibility on his son. He must change his behavior if he wants to enjoy any privileges! It is up to him. You may want to go back and read the dialogue between Tim and Steven at the end of the last chapter to see how Tim introduced the link between these features of responsible choices and privileges.

Focus on the Choices You Can See

Throughout his talk with Steven, Tim made reference to people in the Bible whose choices resulted in privileges or their loss. Tim told Steven that he was going to show him respect as a young adult. Tim was not going to put himself in the position of having to judge Steven's sincerity. He was going to affirm, though, that Steven's choices were real, and he was going to respect them as real.

One of the common responses to this kind of discussion is to accuse mom or dad of not trusting them. It usually shuts the conversation down and gets mom or dad to back away from their discipline. "You don't trust anything I say. That's why I'm so sick of living here. You are suspicious about everything."

It is easy for a parent to take the bait and debate with the teen about trust, explaining that it is something that is won or lost by truthfulness or by a record of responsible behavior. These are all true things to be addressed in time, but in the heat of the moment, you should keep the focus on your teen's choices. Agree that there are times that you have trusted your son and there are times you have not. Sometimes you may have been right and sometimes you may have been wrong. Explain to him that the topic now is not about trusting what his intentions may be but trusting his maturity, his actual choices.

Clarify the difference between trusting his intentions and his maturity. Explain that you can't see his heart and mind and so you cannot judge in that area. You may be deeply suspicious about his motives, but truthfully, you can't see his heart. Mature choices, though, are a different matter. To illustrate, you may want to affirm that you can't even trust yourself to make mature decisions. You need to be held accountable too because you are capable of foolishness and self-destructive behaviors. Use an example of how you allow people (spouse, pastor, small group leader, ministry team leader, Bible teacher, etc.) to keep watch over your choices and to speak into your life if they sense that something might not be quite right. (This will probably take him off guard and help minimize the "you-think-you-are-so-perfect" charge.) You are in the process of growth too. God holds you accountable for your choices too, and he requires that you hold your son or daughter accountable for what you can see, not what you cannot see—his motives and intentions. (I will get into this more when we are talking about holding teens accountable for their attitudes in the next chapter.) The Bible urges all believers to live with accountability among the community of his people, the church. You need that accountability too. That is one of the important reasons that you are part of the church. Your accountability, though, unlike your teen's, includes parenting as God directs.

Our Choices Are Our Own

Choices by definition are intentional decisions. They may be hasty, foolish and sinful, or they may be thoughtful, wise and righteous, but they are all intentional.

We can make choices because we are created in the image of God. The testimony of all Scripture is that our choices are real and God holds us accountable for them. Tim underscored this by citing Galatians 6:7 about sowing and reaping and Proverbs 9:12 about living wisely or mocking authority. In both instances there is either reward for right living or suffering for sowing foolishness. This understanding undermines the legitimacy of any excuses we may be tempted to use to explain away or justify our poor choices, and it also levels the playing field—wrongdoing by anyone is still wrongdoing. No one and no condition ever makes me make a bad decision.

This is not the place to discuss some rare exceptions that include chronic chemical imbalances, genetic deformities, or the like. This book is about angry teens who *can* function normally and make wise decisions and can fit in with expectations adults have for them. They may rage and throw things at home but they more than likely don't do that at a friend's house or in a movie theater. They may use profanity in their anger or defiance at home, but they probably don't do that in school, church, or when their grandparents visit. The testimony of Scripture is that, as a rule, our decisions are intentional and have consequences—positive or negative.

Some Parental Responses to Common Excuses

"Yes, your teacher's impatience might be a problem, but that doesn't justify your wrongdoing. Your teacher is under the authority of her administrator and may need to think about her behavior, but even if she is totally out of line, you are still obligated to speak respectfully to her. Is your response likely to allow you to enjoy privileges and respect at school and here at home or is it likely you've chosen to forfeit some of them?"

This parent isn't "taking sides" with the teacher or the teen. In fact, she is making sure her daughter understands that the teacher could be wrong. Nothing excuses her wrongdoing if she is. But the parent is being just as emphatic about her own daughter's responsibility—regardless of the teacher's wrongdoing. (Of course, we're not talking about a physically abusive teacher. We're talking about a teacher who is requiring her student to behave or comply in some manner that the teen doesn't like.)

"Your mother's questions might annoy you, but your disrespect is wrong regardless of how she talks to you. This doesn't justify any wrongdoing on mom's part, but you can't use her behavior as an excuse for yours. Is this response likely to allow you to enjoy privileges and freedom or is it likely this response is a choice to forfeit some of them?"

This dad is clarifying that moms and dads can be annoying, intrusive and embarrassing. No parents want to be those things. But it happens, and it may make it difficult for a young adult to respond in civil and respectful ways. But respectful responses are exactly what are necessary. The rest of life is going to be made up of responses to people who don't treat you the way you would like.

> "Our rules may be too strict and maybe we should talk about them with you. That is reasonable. We do need to respect your young adult ability to evaluate decisions that we make here at home. But your rage, defiance and anger are wrong regardless of whether or not we end up agreeing about some of these expectations. God will hold us accountable for our parenting, and he says we must do the same with your response to us—regardless of how out of touch we may seem to you. Is this response likely to allow you to enjoy privileges and freedom or is it likely this response is a choice to forfeit some of them?"

These parents are acknowledging their teen's ability to think and make decisions about how things are going at home. They are also reiterating the theme that they are accountable just as their teen is—regardless of whether or not they end up agreeing.

Young adults are as adept at excuse-making and rationalizing as we older adults are. It comes with our twisted human nature that distorts our thinking and feeds our self-centeredness. Proverbs 13:10 affirms the source of contention, quarrels and strife:

"By insolence comes nothing but strife" (ESV & NASB).

"Pride only breeds quarrels" (NIV, 1984).

"Only by pride cometh contention" (KJV).

None of our teen's efforts to blame others or excuse themselves may be allowed to stand and exempt them from the pain and loss that comes from unwise choices.

Our Consequences Are Linked to Our Choices

In the last chapter we summarized a number of people in the Old and New Testaments who illustrated the loss of privileges because of their choices. God held them accountable. This pattern was important enough for Paul to draw special attention to the Corinthian church about some of their risky choices. In the very next chapter after his warning, he illustrates the way some of the Corinthians themselves have been affected by the pain and loss of God's discipline in the church.

Paul shows that Israel's experience of loss is an example for his New Testament people to be on guard against the subtlety and deceitfulness of idolatry—taking their cues for living from any authority other than their Lord.

> Now these things took place as examples for us, that we might not desire evil as they did. Do not be idolaters as some of them were; as it is written, "The people sat down to eat and drink and rose up to play." We must not indulge in sexual immorality as some of them did, and twenty-three thousand fell in a single day. We must not put Christ to the test, as some of them did and were destroyed by serpents, nor grumble, as some of them did and were destroyed by the Destroyer. Now these things happened to them as an example, but they were written down for our instruction, on whom the end of the ages has come.
>
> —1 Corinthians 10:6–11

Their idolatry showed up in their "desire" for evil, their revelry and partying, their sexual immorality and their grumbling and complaining spirits. Some became ill and some died. They lost every benefit that had been promised because of their folly.

Pain and Loss of Privileges for Foolish Choices Are the Father's Training Wheels

I've had the opportunity to teach all six of our kids to ride a bike—most of them have used training wheels to help them with balance when they started. In time, I took the training wheels off and then ran alongside their bikes to help them with balance till they got the hang of it.

Experiencing loss is like those training wheels. Loss (of health, things, relationships, opportunities, etc.) gives us, at any age, the occasion to reflect on and reorder our priorities so that they can be aligned with God's wise will for our lives. Loss helps us restore balance to an otherwise skewed set of priorities. Solomon observes this connection between choices and outcomes, "Good sense wins favor, but the way of the treacherous is their ruin" (Proverbs 13:15).

A lifestyle that conforms to God's righteous, wise counsel in his word will usually win favor among people and be to our advantage. *Ruin*, on the other hand, typically follows living without concern for God's wise counsel. *Ruin* in this verse is sometimes translated "rugged" or "hard." That lifestyle will usually bring one into tough, rugged, difficult times, times of loss of one form or another. Our commission to parent includes imitating our heavenly Parent's example with our teens to help them reflect and realign their priorities.

Respecting Our Teen Means Linking Our Love with His Loss Because of His Choices

We must respect our teens because God has created them in his image and has commanded us to do so. Loving our neighbor as our selves, the second great commandment, includes seeking the well-being of our young adult. Until our teens display a pattern of wise and respectful behaviors and attitudes, we are obligated to imitate our Father's disciplinary pattern to allow pain to come into their lives—especially the pain of loss. We'll illustrate more of this connection in the chapters that follow.

We need to be reminded of this link between teen choices and outcomes, or we can be easily seduced by our world's sentimental view that says our teens are entitled to the stuff that the culture loves to advertise as things that we need. They *need* their iPod, iPad, laptop, Facebook, their own car, HDTV, fashionable clothes, their own space, free time, their own room, their own money, their privacy. The list goes on and as the culture continues to change so will the "needs" that teens are told they have.

When a mother came to me for help with her teen's unwillingness to do homework, she told me she didn't know how to motivate him. "When I come home from work, there he is in the living room watching TV. I tell him to turn off the TV and do his homework, but he just says he will do it later. If I turn off the TV, he gets mad and goes to his room and watches the TV in his room. I don't know what to do!"

This may seem like an extreme example, but, sadly, it's not uncommon in today's culture of entitledness. Parents can easily be seduced into believing that luxuries and privileges are things that their teens deserve and need. "After all, don't our teens have a "right" to their own money? They worked for it, so how can I tell them what they must do with it?"

The way of the treacherous or unfaithful is their ruin. This kind of life is hard. It's the weight and burden of a hard life that Jesus invited people to abandon when he called on them to "Come to me, all who labor and are heavy laden, and I will give you rest" (Matthew 11:28). Your teen is similarly weighed down, whether he acknowledges it right now or not. The measures of accountability you are going to allow to come his way will add to that heaviness so much that he won't be able to easily ignore it. This is a good thing. It is this pain that may be used by God to break the fantasy about his "rights" and clarify the connection his privileges have with responsible living—inside and outside of your home, now and for eternity.

Conclusion

It was Tim's intention to allow Steven to sink deeper in the waters of willfulness and to become frustrated, distressed and free of every idol that he had clung to as his entitlements. That is how he prayed for Steven. Extracting the idols from his heart would be a work that only the Spirit of God could do. He had his role as a parent. But the desired repentance and change from the heart was something only God could do.

While talking about choices, Tim was lacing his talk with lots of hope. Change is something Steven could do *if he wanted to*. That's what the options for wise and foolish choices assume. Steven wasn't locked into some prison of lost hope. Not yet, anyway. Such a time could come according to Proverbs 29:1. "He who is often reproved, yet stiffens his neck, will suddenly be broken beyond healing." Some stubbornness and willfulness can result in one being broken beyond healing. Others, however, heed the reproof and turn from their ways to God-pleasing decisions. Part of the reason Tim was engaged in this discussion with Steven was to warn him that his choices could lead to a more fatal outcome. He wanted Steven to feel the pain and loss of his folly now in order to make the connection between his choices and their consequences so that he wouldn't become one who is stiff-necked later in his life.

Some teens have their heels "dug in." "It doesn't matter what you do to me, I'm not going to . . ." ("talk the way you want me to," "show you any respect," "go back to that school," "get out of bed," "talk to her ever again," etc.). Such a teen may have to experience the pain of very serious loss. We'll address that in chapters ahead. But the young person who understands that his choices are his own and that God has designed life so that sooner or later loss or difficult times usually follow foolish choices will often begin to change his behavior. That's been the testimony of many who have seen their prodigal teen return after getting a snoot full of this world's emptiness and a body scarred by its ruggedness. That is what happened to the prodigal son who left his perfectly parented home to pursue his idolatries. He "squandered his property in reckless living" (Luke 15:13). But it was the losses in his life that brought him "to himself" (v. 17), both spiritually and rationally. This doesn't mean there are not long-lasting effects from poor choices. As we saw earlier many sins can result in enduring pain. Adam and Eve's sin has enduring consequences for the entire human race. David never got to see his little son grow and mature. He died as a consequence of David's immorality with Bathsheba. But even these outcomes, in the hands of a gracious and good Father, will be used for "good" in the life of believers who entrust themselves to Him (see Romans 8:28). More of that hope will follow in our last chapters.

10

MAKE THE WATER DEEPEST

BY IDENTIFYING RESPECTFUL AND RESPONSIBLE ATTITUDES

Everyone who is angry with his brother will be liable to judgment; whoever insults his brother will be liable to the council.

—Matthew 5:22

God delivers some of his most violent expressions for judgment for young people with scornful or mocking attitudes. "The eye that mocks a father and scorns to obey a mother will be picked out by the ravens of the valley and eaten by the vultures" (Proverbs 30:17). In Proverbs, "mocker," "scorner" and "scoffer" are used interchangeably and by different translators to refer to the same person who has attitudes of dishonor, disrespect and contempt for others, especially people in authority over them.

Attitudes are forms of communication. They are chosen behaviors, too. But they are not always audible; they are not necessarily spoken. We can communicate them either verbally or nonverbally with body language, especially by our tone of voice or our facial expressions.

The smirk, or pursed lips, rolling eyes and deep sigh are some of the most common forms in which attitudes of contempt are shown. But our sinful hearts are creative and we and our angry teens can find other ways to make defiant, dishonoring statements without using words. The silent treatment, the glaring look, refusing to look at one who is speaking, refusing to answer, walking away when being spoken to, the disrespectful "why?" (which isn't really a question but is a rhetorical statement that is saying, "This is stupid! You don't make any sense. I shouldn't have to do anything you say!") The list of expressions of contempt for your authority or anyone's under whom God has placed the teen goes on and on.

There are several factors about attitudes and the angry, willful teen that come into play for any parents who are seeking to be faithful to the Lord in their parenting. I will touch on four of them here. I've written other books[8] that go into more detail about attitudes if you are interested, but here I will give a biblical overview of attitudes.

1. Angry, Defiant Attitudes Are Like Murder!

It is true that attitudes are not as easily identifiable as cursing, throwing the TV remote, smashing a phone, punching a hole in a wall or breaking a window. Just because attitudes are tough to get a hold of doesn't mean that parents should ignore them. Just because angry attitudes are internal doesn't mean they are less destructive. Jesus called anger a form of murder.

> You have heard that it was said to those of old, 'You shall not murder; and whoever murders will be liable to judgment.' But I say to you that everyone who is angry with his brother will be liable to judgment; whoever insults his brother will be liable to the council; and whoever says, 'You fool!' will be liable to the hell of fire.
>
> —Matthew 5:21–22

Jesus was exploding the Jewish teaching that sin is only one's external behavior. Certainly physical murder is sin. But so are an internal spirit of anger, a verbal insult and an attitude of contempt that shows up in the example of one's disposition by calling another person a "fool." All these are expressions of murder by Jesus' definition.

James said that "whoever keeps the whole law but fails in one point has become accountable for all of it" (James 2:10). He later showed that anger is a form of violence in his epistle and says the angry, demanding spirits of his readers cause quarrels and fights among them. He told his audience "You desire and do not have, so you murder" (James 4:2). These people were not literally killing each other. But they were destroying relationships and the character God wanted them to cultivate by their bitterness, anger and resentment because, as James said, "you covet and cannot obtain, so you fight and quarrel."

Isn't that what our angry, bitter teens are doing? If not with words, they fight us with their attitudes of contempt because they want something that they have been told they can't have. Their attitudes are not benign growths. They are aggressive cancers seeking to destroy—they are forms of murder.

2. God Requires Accountability for Attitudes of Contempt

God is offended when young adults have attitudes of contempt for authority. As we saw at the beginning of the chapter, Agur, the author of Proverbs 30, identifies the eye as the offending member of the body that mocks a father, not the tongue. Tongues can offend and dishonor, but oftentimes it's the eye that reveals our attitudes.

Attitudes can be slippery and hard to get a firm grasp on. Yet it is clear from Proverbs 30:17 that God has a strong opinion about them and expects parents who follow him to address them. He wants them to be just as serious about confronting attitudes of contempt as he is. God holds scorners and mockers accountable and he expects parents to do the same.

Below is a series of proverbs that address attitudes. Notice the verbs (in bold) that describe the actions parents and other authorities are to take when facing teens with attitudes of contempt. Notice too, the reactions (*in italics*) of the young adults and scoffers:

Whoever **corrects** a scoffer gets himself *abuse*, and he who **reproves** a wicked man *incurs injury*. Do not **reprove** a scoffer or he will *hate* you. (9:7, 8)

A wise son hears his father's **instruction**, but a scoffer *does not listen* to **rebuke**. (13:1)

A scoffer *does not like* to be **reproved**; he *will not go to the wise*. (15:12)

Strike a scoffer, and the simple will learn prudence. (19:25)

When a scoffer is **punished**, the simple become wise. (21:11)

Drive out a scoffer, and strife will go out, and *quarreling and abuse will cease*. (22:10)

Scoffers *set a city aflame*, but the wise **turn away wrath**. (29:8)

"Correct," "reprove," "instruct," "rebuke," "strike," "punish" and even the extreme "drive out" are given as directives to parents of children who display attitudes of mockery or scorn—contempt for authority. These attitudes are dishonoring to God and parents, and hurtful, destructive and dangerously infectious to others.

There are certainly times and ways in which a literal application of these concepts is appropriate. But the bottom line is that parents are to use some form of disciplinary pain to let the young adult know that his spirit is wrong, his attitudes are disrespectful, and are just as virulent as any violent outbreaks with words or destructive behavior. In biblical times these "strike," "punish" and "cast-out" varieties of discipline were often literally applied.

But so were the less dramatic more verbal forms of "correct," "instruct," "reprove" and "rebuke." This entire range of interventions is at the disposal of parents—to address destructive attitudes, not just violent words and actions.

3. We Choose Our Attitudes

Everybody chooses the attitude they are going to show to the authorities in their lives. This perspective may not be culturally popular, or acceptable to many in the professional therapeutic community, but it is biblically accurate. Children and adults alike *choose* to have attitudes of either honor or contempt toward the authorities in their lives. Their identity as people created in the image of God gives them that capability.

Go back and review the verses from Proverbs in the last section. Notice the absence of excuses or explanations for *why* the young person was a scoffer or mocker. Many of our young people have terrible experiences. Many of these troubles are not due to any fault of their own. They live in a broken world and sometimes it breaks on them in tragic and horrible ways: dysfunction, divorce, exploitation, injustice, bullying, the list goes on. These are serious abuses and should not be casually dismissed. They should be addressed with mercy and love. But they do not, as the Bible illustrates time and again, *cause* someone to choose sinful attitudes or actions in response to their suffering.

Some time ago an African American mother brought her tenth grade son into my office. He was angry because his history and English teachers had not given significant attention to African American historic figures, but neither his mother nor I knew that at first. Instead of addressing his feelings in a respectful way, he chose to have a belligerent and contemptuous attitude, which ended up affecting his grades. I asked one of the teachers to join us and then asked the young man what he thought was causing his trouble in class. He quickly began to criticize the teacher.

"This is Black History month and he (pointing to his teacher) has done absolutely nothing to address any black figures in history. He . . ."

"You stop right now!" his mother interrupted. "You will not talk to your teacher that way. You will show him respect. Even if he is wrong, you will show him respect! Do you hear me?! Attitude determines altitude," she concluded.

Her son immediately changed his tone and his facial expression from an attack mode to one of humility. The teacher acknowledged his oversight and apologized, promising to address the problem.

What impressed me more was the mother's reply when the teacher apologized and indicated his willingness to address the topic. "I appreciate that," she said, "but that is not necessary in order for my son to present himself better in your class and to do his work acceptably. He must have a respectful attitude toward you, and if he does not, I want you to let me know. Is that okay with you?"

The culture, other people, family conditions, personal experiences and our own parenting all affect our children and teens to be sure. But the affirmation throughout Scripture is that, ultimately, people make their own choices about the attitudes and behaviors they are going to adopt. Attitudes are chosen. They may be related to the way others are treating us but they are not *caused* by outside forces in our broken world.

Some time ago I was part of a student-faculty talent show in our school. I was cast as a villain. We practiced in a classroom and I used a piece of chalk for a knife, an imaginary rope to tie up a prisoner, a blackboard eraser as a gun—all substitute props. We had no stage or set for our practice times, just the classroom with the chairs and desks shoved aside. On the day before the melodrama talent show production, we actually rehearsed on stage with the set and real look-alike props, a rubber knife, plastic gun and a real rope. Probably because I'm not much of an actor, I found it much easier to get in character with all the staging and props. The set made it easier. It didn't make me act any better but it did invite me to put myself into the role more aggressively.

That's what the troubles and hardships, abuse and mistreatment that we and our teens experience do to us. They don't *make* us respond in anger and defiance or make us have dispositions of contempt, bitterness, resentment or vindictiveness. But they may make it easier for us to exhibit them. We make choices to respond in these ways. We are not made to do so. That's why Jesus taught that all such expressions, internal and external, are destructive and are violations of the command to not murder.

4. Attitudes Are Detectable

Common statistics about communication assert that we communicate only 7 percent with words, 38 percent with tone of voice and 55 percent by facial or other nonverbal expressions. Angry teens know they can communicate without words too. They provide clues to their attitudes. They may mope, slouch, smirk or smile at what others would consider inappropriate times, or most commonly, they may roll their eyes and sigh at something they don't like. Parents should not allow or ignore a scorning or dishonoring attitude any more than they should allow their teens to lie, use vulgar language or take the Lord's name in vain.

Keep three things in mind when addressing bad attitudes: 1) look for patterns, 2) verify the clues with your teen and 3) confirm your judgment with others.

First, look for patterns. Scornful, disrespectful attitudes may not be as obvious as other defiant actions, but they are detectable. A rare display of an attitude of impatience or contempt, while wrong, is not necessarily identifying your teen as a scorner as Proverbs describes. The scorner is one who frequently displays contempt for your authority as a pattern of behavior. While occasional scornful expressions should be addressed as sin too, it's the pattern of clues that marks a scorner or scoffer. It's the pattern that we must identify. That pattern often shows up in teens marked by angry, defiant willful dispositions.

Second, verify the clues you witness with your teen. You should be sure about what you are seeing. You can't see his heart, though you may have a pretty good idea about what is in there. To confirm your suspicions, talk to your teen. Instead of accusing your teen of what you think is going on in his heart or getting into an interpretive war about what his attitude is tell your teen what his nonverbal clues—his smirk, rolling eyes, silence—are saying *to you,* not what the teen means by it. "I don't know what is in your heart, Steven, but your tone and the smirk on your face when I'm talking to you is saying volumes to me. It tells me that you do not respect the position God has given us as your parents or the responsibility he entrusts to us to give you guidance in life matters or to manage our home. You are saying things like this without ever speaking a word."

"You are judging me! You don't know what I'm thinking. The Bible says don't judge people. That's what you're doing."

"Steven, I don't know what is in your heart. I am not a mind reader. I can't say you are intending to dishonor me or mom. But your tone and your face convey disrespect whether you want to show that or not. That is what must change. If you intend dishonor to us in your heart, that is a private matter between you and God. You are right, I can't detect that or do anything about it. But your display of that attitude is what I'm saying must change."

Identify clearly the *behaviors* that communicate to you a dishonoring spirit. These could include nonverbal clues (such as slamming the door, stomping out of the room, not looking at you when you are talking to him) or verbal clues (like interrupting or arguing with you in a belittling, defiant or disrespectful tone.) Your teen doesn't have to agree that they are being disrespectful. Most of the time, if she is a scorner, she won't agree. That's her character. They do not listen to rebuke or instruction or correction. Nevertheless, you must hold the line. God gives parents the ability to discern whether the spirit they are seeing in their teen is wholesome or hurtful. He has also given them the responsibility to confront their young adult when it is the latter.

Remember, just as you must not allow forms of verbal contempt—defiant speech, vulgarity or profanity—to go unchecked, neither should you allow to go unchecked attitudes of contempt, which the teen expresses with his body language or tone of voice.

That brings us to the third thing to keep in mind when addressing bad attitudes. In order to be accurate you should confirm your suspicions with others. You may not be able to see your son's heart exactly. But you can see what comes out of his heart, and you can confirm what you are seeing by talking to others who witness the same expressions.

Most of the time, you are observing a pattern. By the time you meet to talk to your teen about his behavior and to connect it to his choices, you will have seen your teen's disrespectfulness repeatedly. As you begin to suspect that there is a problem, confer with your spouse or youth leaders at church or teachers in his school. The people in authority in your teen's life are the ones who see most clearly the bad attitudes of his heart. The clues displayed to others may not be as dramatic or flagrant as the ones exhibited to you, but you want to confirm that what you are seeing is, in fact, disrespectful and dishonoring, a form of contempt or anger for you and your parental role.

Conclusion

Your angry or willful teen has made you the "bad guy." He's been accustomed to feeling secure with his attitudes and self-centered way of living because he hasn't been in over his head yet. Addressing the concepts of privileges, responsible choices and respectful attitudes will be an announcement to him that things are going to change.

He has privileges but no rights! His wise behavioral choices will now be connected to the privileges he does have. His attitudes are part of his behavioral choices that you will take into account and that will be connected to his privileges.

In the final chapter of this section, we'll look at how to actually give your teen the pain and let him sink in over his head. Like all other sections of this book, this must be approached prayerfully and thoughtfully. The goal is to bring your daughter to a deep-water experience so that she will find herself at the end of her rope, just as the prodigal son experienced, so that she comes to enjoy the Father's embrace and celebration. Pray that the Lord will use your spirit, your words and your decisions for accountability to produce that end.

11

DEVELOP YOUR PLAN TO SHEPHERD YOUR TEEN INTO DEEP WATER

When the Spirit of truth comes, he will guide you into all the truth, for he will not speak on his own authority, but whatever he hears he will speak, and he will declare to you the things that are to come.

—John 16:13

In the last three chapters I showed you how to take your teen into deep waters by explaining the principles of privileges, respectfulness and accountability, and letting him know that you are going to hold him to a higher standard. He will likely be disorientated and, perhaps, more angry, but he will definitely sense that you are taking charge of your home. This is his deep-water situation, one that he's not use to.

In this chapter I suggest some specific ways to prepare and to discuss your plan for change with your teen. I'm using the term *discuss* loosely. The fact is, often when a teen with a defiant spirit gets a sense that the conversation is going to be about his behavior or responsibilities, it becomes a one-way conversation. You end up doing all the talking. That is okay for now. You are announcing a change or a different emphasis in your parenting strategy to him. He's going to have to process what he hears after the smoke of his anger clears. He is going to hear how some of what he's taken for granted as his rights have just become linked to responsible and respectful behavior.

How to Prepare for the "Discussion"

Pray for your upcoming conversation. We can never pray too much. You have probably been lifting your situation to the throne of grace quite often. Make an effort now to pray with your spouse and others in your church community for God to work in your teen's life and your own hearts with more attention to each of the features we've talked about in this book.

- Pray that the Lord will help you keep the big, God-glorifying picture in mind throughout your conversation.

- Pray for the undertow forces of your own heart that we addressed earlier.

- Pray for the specifics of the plan that you are thinking about.

- Pray that you and your spouse will be on the same page.

- Pray for the timing of your conversation.

- Pray for the Holy Spirit's presence in the middle of your conversation.

- Pray for the Spirit to give your teen a humble, repentant spirit.

- Pray for humility, boldness, clarity and love in your conversation with your teen.

- Pray for grace to respond with Christlike love to whatever reaction your teen has.

Pray for the consistency to follow-up on the measures of accountability you are putting in place.

Pray for the grace to respond to others, including believers, who think you are going about this all wrong. (There will probably be some—most of whom have never had a child with this disposition and who may think they have this parenting thing down pat.)

Pray for God to be exalted and glorified through this trial and in the long term in the lives of your family members.

Pray for the grace and faith to keep a long-term perspective in view and to radiate the genuine joy of the Lord in the midst of the trial.

We'll revisit some of these requests in the last section of this book when we address God's grace to parents in the midst of this storm.

Decide what must change first. There may be dozens of things you believe must change about your teen's words, behaviors and attitudes. You are probably right in thinking so. They certainly need to change. But pattern the training of your teen after the way Jesus trained his disciples. He paced his training of them. At one point he made it clear that he had more to teach them but they were not ready for it yet. "I still have many things to say to you, but you cannot bear them now" (John 16:12). He then went on to say that the Spirit of truth would continue what he had begun and "guide you into all the truth" (16:13). God is beginning this task with you as a primary agent. But as in all of our cases, God has much more to do in us and in our teen, and, over time, he'll use other agents by his Spirit to accomplish his mission.

When you pray with your spouse and other brothers and sisters in the church, pray about what two or three things you are going to insist must change immediately. Is it vulgarity, profanity or misusing the Lord's name? Is it violent outbursts? Is it not speaking when spoken to? Is it leaving the house without permission or not returning to the house by the curfew time? Some less dramatic patterns of irresponsible behavior that may be defiant and willful include things like not doing home chores without complaining, not being on time in the morning to leave for school, not doing homework and turning it in on time, and not getting off the phone when told to do so. You'll need to determine which few things to address first in your situation. But limit your requirements to just a few at the start. Change is a process, and there is a lifetime in which to do it.

Develop a simple plan. The simpler the plan the better—and not just for your teen. Don't forget, you must monitor the plan. Your teen is going to need to be held accountable for her behavior. Not everything you have done has been a failure. She has made and is making her own choices and is responsible for them. But what needs to change is your determination, by the grace of God, to now hold her accountable. You will need to attach privileges to her positive behavior, her respectful words and attitudes. But in order for this to happen, you must change things you do in order to hold her accountable and monitor your plan. If the plan is too complicated it will be hard for you to remember it and be consistent in adhering to it. Make the plan simple so you can keep up with the demands that your part in the change will require.

A number of years ago, a single mother contacted me about her ninth grade son's foul language. She said she had no way to keep him from using profanity when he got mad and wondered if the school could help her.

Her desire was clear—no foul language. We defined what words she wanted to curb in graphic detail—mostly four and five letter words. She wanted her home to honor the Lord and for friends of her other children to be able to be there and not be subjected to this language.

The specific plan we came up with might not fly today, but it did at that time. Any day Anton used foul language at home, she was to call me. The next day I would mobilize a "team" of three big men (other teachers) who would remove him from his class, take him to the locker room and wash his mouth out with a disgusting, gag-inducing bar of soap. His mom was totally committed to this plan.

His mom and I met with Anton. I explained very clearly that if he used foul language as defined by the words his mother gave him, he could expect the team to show up sometime during the day to escort him to the locker room where they would wash his mouth out with soap. But if he used good language, he would be soap free. The choice was his.

For most of the first week Anton was a model son at home. Then he let a string of profanities fly at his mom because she would not let him do something he wanted to do. His mom called me, and the next morning I mobilized the team. We met Anton on his way to second period and escorted him to the locker room. He came along willingly. We were all bigger than Anton, but a couple guys were much bigger. There was no violence. He took it willingly (Maybe he was glad to have men in his life who cared. I'm not sure.) He gagged, threw up a little and cleaned up. We talked a few minutes, prayed together and then he went back to class.

Anton never lost his temper with his language again that school year!

Anton's mom's plan was simple and easy for her, and us, to enforce.

Another mom was having trouble getting her son Jeremy out of bed in the mornings and to school on time. His dad usually left for work before the rest of the family was up. Jeremy began dragging his feet early in the school year when his mom would call to get him up. He'd finally get up when it was too late to catch the bus. If he did get up, he'd go in the bathroom and close the door and stay in there until it was too late to catch the bus. When his mom would drive him to school, he would refuse to get out of the car.

Jeremy was in ninth grade, and he was a big boy, both tall and stout. She came in to see me because he had missed so many days of school in the first half of the year that he was in danger of not moving on to the next grade. After talking about the possibilities of holding Jeremy accountable, I quoted 2 Thessalonians 3:10: "if anyone is not willing to work, let him not eat." I knew from looking at him, that Jeremy liked to eat. His mom immediately got an idea. Since school was his work, she figured that if he didn't come to school he shouldn't eat another meal until he returned from school the next day. I thought it was a great idea. The privilege of eating was attached to his coming to school.

Jeremy's mom went home and explained the plan. Since he had missed school that day, he didn't get any lunch or dinner that day and no breakfast the next morning. (She had to camp out in the kitchen, but she was willing to do that to make this work.) She packed a lunch for him to take the next morning but he ate it on the way to school. He was famished. That was okay. The next meal he'd get would be dinner. His mother's plan was simple. She attached the privilege of eating to his responsible actions. Though it was inconvenient to stay in the kitchen that first day and evening, it was a plan that she could easily enforce. Jeremy did not miss another day the rest of the school year.

In our ongoing story about Tim and Steven, Tim put all three of these principles into action: Prayer, Deciding what should change first, a simple Plan to link Steven's choices to privileges he enjoyed—but had come to think of as rights.

He and his wife began a regular prayer time right after dinner each evening. They reviewed their goals and asked the Lord to help them both be in agreement and to communicate humility, love and righteousness to Steven. They reviewed each of the topics above to seek the Father's guidance and the Spirit's power. Most of all they prayed for a spirit of repentance in Steven.

Tim and his wife decided that the first thing they were going to address was Steven's language, his vulgarity, profanity and misuse of the Lord's name. A second issue they would address was Steven's violent outbursts at home, such as slamming a door, throwing something or destroying something.

Their plan would be to link Steven's bad language to his privileges of being with and communicating with his friends. His respectful communication at home would give him the privilege to go out with his friends and send text messages and be on Facebook. If he chose to be disrespectful at home with his language, he was saying that he was willing to give up his time with his friends and his phone and computer for the next week. He would determine the level of freedom he'd have. And for his outbursts, they were going to start deducting money from his savings to pay for the repairs for anything he damaged.

By setting up the link between Steven's behavior at home and the privileges he enjoyed, Tim and his wife let Steven know that when he acted up at home it was sending a statement that he did not want the privileges of being with and communicating with his friends or spending his money in ways he would like. They told him that when he began to feel his temper rise, he should leave the situation and get alone to get control by reminding himself of the privileges he wanted to keep access to. His self-control at home in these two areas would show that he could be trusted to exercise self-control away from home and would allow him to enjoy privileges that they linked to his behavior.

Having a simple plan is important and will often put teens in water over their heads and make them gasp for relief—sometimes sooner and sometimes later. As we'll see in the next chapters, this does not always happen quickly and may involve years of waiting, praying and staying the painful course at home.

Arrange to review your plan after two weeks. From the outset, keep the possibility in mind that it may be wise to modify your plan after a few weeks. You should begin your conversation with a firm plan in mind. This is what is to be practiced for the next two or three weeks, without exception. But it may give some hope to your teen, some sense of control, if he sees that even the plan is moldable according to the respectful quality of his choices. Of course the plans should also be modified if the sting of losses he is suffering doesn't seem to be motivating him to change ungodly, hurtful behavior in your home.

Tim was able to present his plan to Steven with this measure of hopefulness embedded in it. After three weeks he and Steven's mom would talk to him about ways his behavior has freed him to enjoy some privileges of communication and to be out with friends. They'd ask him for ways he thought the plan could be adapted to allow him to show even greater maturity in both of these areas, his language and his outbursts.

Tim and his wife were not obligated to do what Steven suggested, but they would be asking for his input. This gave a measure of hope to Steven when his dad presented the plan to him and after his initial anger subsided as he reflected on the possibilities in the weeks to come.

These four suggestions are for preparation *before you meet* to discuss the plan. Two other suggestions can help make your "speech judicious" and add "persuasiveness to [your] lips" (Proverbs 16:23).

The "Discussion"

Timing is important. You've prayed about the timing of your conversation. Timing is critical for effective communication. "Whoever blesses his neighbor with a loud voice, rising early in the morning, will be counted as cursing" (Proverbs 27:14). Blessing someone is good. Doing it loudly can even be very honoring. But doing it loudly early in the morning, that is very different. "Let me alone. Let me sleep. At least let me wake up and have my first cup of coffee." What was intended to be a good thing most likely will be interpreted as cursing.

You want your plan to result in blessing. The likelihood is that your teen won't see it that way at the outset. So your approach and timing is even more important than the guy who was blessing his neighbor early in the morning. No matter what you do, your conversation may be interpreted as a curse.

Plan to have your conversation when tempers are cool, when neither one of you is in a hurry, when you are not hungry or tired and when there is minimal ice in the air. If these circumstances don't show up in your home, tell your teen that you want to set a time with him to have a conversation "about some thinking you have been doing about your home." The meeting doesn't have to be convenient for him. If he is never willing to meet with you to talk, you take the initiative to get with him. The conversation is urgent. Do the best you can to arrange a good, welcoming timing, but if that is not possible, forge ahead as respectfully and as clearly as you can.

Explain your plan clearly and ask your teen to repeat its key points back to you. He may or may not say anything. Approach this part of your conversation with prayerful humility and sensitivity. Your teen is "going under" and may begin to feel overwhelmed and confused. That can be very good. He's been giving the pain to every one else in the household, and now he's about to be an object of affliction—of his own making.

In review of the details I outline above, keep in mind the following:

- **Be confident** that your concern is God's concern.
- **Affirm your respect** for your teen as a young adult, and for his freedom to change or not change.
- **Be specific** with the kind of behavior that you are linking to his privileges and the troublesome behavior that needs to change which will cause him to forfeit them.
- **Affirm your motives** are for God's glory, the family's health, and his growth--not your reputation.
- **Explain your plan** by connecting your teen's behavior with his privileges. "As you are respectful by your (name the behavior you want to see) you will be able to enjoy the privilege of (name the privilege that is attached to a pattern of respect)."
- **Keep your plan open to review.** Explain to your teen that in two weeks, if the plan hasn't been working well, you can talk about how it could be modified to help him to be

respectful and cooperative and enjoy more of the privileges available to him.

What will this look like with a strongly defiant, angry, willful teen? That is what I will illustrate in the next chapter. Keep in mind, this book is not written to provide the "silver bullet" for any family. Change that will occur by using any biblical principles will only be enduring change if the Holy Spirit is in the words and in the people. He uses parental planting and watering to get his job done, as Paul asserts when he instructs parents to bring up their children "in the discipline and instruction of the Lord" (Ephesians 6:4). But he also soberly reminds us of our limitations. We can't manufacture the change we long to see, for "neither he who plants nor he who waters is anything, but only God who gives the growth" (1 Corinthians 3:7).

PART 4

OUR STORY

"You make him glad with the joy of your presence."
—Psalm 21:6

"I have no good apart from you."
—Psalm 16:2

"In your presence there is fullness of joy; at your right hand are pleasures forevermore."
—Psalm 16:11

"You're a youth counselor, and you have a kid like that!"

"You do family counseling and speak about youth parenting in conferences, and one of your own teenagers acts out like that!"

"You are a pastor and Bible teacher, and you have a teen who did that!"

For thirty-eight years I've worked with the teenagers of others. I've taught them and counseled them and their parents mostly in Christian school and church contexts. I had a lot more answers to other people's parenting problems when Betty and I were much younger and had only elementary school–aged children.

151

But nothing prepared us for the earthshaking trauma that rocked our family world when our oldest son crashed into his high school years. I say crashed because this was not a smooth transitional time. It was a noisy, bumpy, turbulent and often violent time. You'll get a sense of that in the chapter to follow.

But this was not a tragedy. It certainly felt like one much of the time and looked like one more than we wished it would. But it was what the Lord appointed for us out of his goodness and love. It was what he'd use in our lives and would come to use in the lives of others who were walking on a similar path.

Our Father's chief work was what he was doing in Betty and me. That work is not finished with the publication of this book. We're learning, as the title of the last chapter indicates. Our prayer is that the weaknesses we've exhibited through these years and the story of God's gracious help to us will encourage you to make your Father your ultimate source of joy and delight, as we've been growing to do.

This story has no happy *ending* because the story is not finished yet. What it does have is a rich present work of God's grace and mercy in us and others in our family. May our gracious Father enable you to find the same joy the psalmist echoes in the verses above—not in your circumstances, your success, your ministry, your reputation, your model family or your all-together example but in Christ alone; in God's presence.

Psalm 21:6 was written in reference to David, to David's messianic descendant and the Messiah's own people as his descendants—you and me in Christ. It was written while the fires of opposition still burned against David. It was written for soldiers in the field with some victories under their belts but still in the conflict. It was written for those with "enemies" (v. 8) who "hate" (v. 8), "plan evil" (v. 11), and "devise mischief" (v. 11) against you. If you live with an angry teen, you know the words and works that can come out of this same kind of oppositional spirit that David also faced. Yet he was glad with the joy of God's personal presence in his life.

May these chapters help you find the kind of gladness that will transcend whatever happens in your angry teen's life in the future. The battlefield, the assaults and wounds do not have to determine your joy and contentment. "In your presence there is fullness of joy; at your right hand are pleasures forevermore" (Psalm 16:11).

12

DEEP, DEEPER AND DEEPEST WATER IN OUR HOUSEHOLD

All discipline seems painful rather than pleasant, but later it yields the peaceful fruit of righteousness to those who have been trained by it.

—Hebrews 12:11

It was Father's Day!

Jed[9] was standing in our garage holding a gas can and a lighter. He was threatening to burn the garage down. He was sick of this house. Sick of these rules. Tired of these restrictions. I stood pleading with him to put the lighter and the gasoline down.

The special Father's Day dinner had started out fine. Our kids were back from college for the weekend so we had a table full—six kids, a couple of boyfriends, some close friends from church and Betty and I. We were sitting around the table at the beginning of our dinner. I had just given thanks for the food and the company. The meal had begun. Everyone was in a festive mood—except Jed. Jed is one of our two adopted African American boys. He'd been part of the family since he was four months old. At the time he was a six foot two inch fifteen-year-old eighth grader. His four sisters and younger brother were all enjoying eating mom's home cooking—especially the college students. Jed got up from the table headed for the kitchen. Betty asked Jed to get the salt and pepper while he was up.

"No, I'm not getting anything for you!"

I turned to him and told him to change his tone toward his mother and to do as he was asked. He just glared at me and said he'd do what he wanted to do. I got up and followed him into the kitchen. He picked up a knife from the counter and turned toward me. I tried to talk to him, but he walked down the steps to a landing to the back screen door and onto the patio. He warned me to keep away, but I followed him anyway. He didn't want any sermons, he said. I moved toward the door, and he slashed at it with the knife, cutting the screen. He moved down the sidewalk and stepped into the garage, picked up a gasoline can and pulled a lighter out of his pocket, threatening to spray the gas and light it.

"Jed, think about what you are doing."

"I hate it here! I'm just sick of you guys always telling me what to do."

"Jed, what about your dreams to play basketball, work with children, which you are so good at doing, and have a family of your own? You are on the verge of throwing all of that away."

"I don't care about any of that, now. I just want to leave here."

Deep Water

Until the end of his seventh grade year, Jed and I had a very strong and close relationship. He was also close to his mom. Sure, there were a lot of contests of the wills when he was growing up:

"Jed, please move those toys out of the reach of your younger brother."

"Jed, don't touch the electric receptacle with the clothes hanger."

"Jed, put all the toys back in the playroom."

"Jed, please take your sneakers to the back landing."

His strong will tested us over the silliest, most unimportant things. Jed lost privileges like a Christmas tree loses its dry needles after the holiday. Often, though, that didn't matter to Jed. He had a high tolerance for pain, physical or otherwise.

It wasn't until the end of middle school, however, that he took his strong willfulness and defiance to a new level. Even today, Jed isn't really sure why he did what he did. "It wasn't you guys, it was me," he says. He really has no explanation for his acting out.

There were many nights in which I went to Jed's room after 10:00 p.m. to try to talk to him about his angry outbursts and general nastiness. Many times he used vulgar and profane language toward me or his mother when we tried to reason with him. The only recourse I had on many of these evenings when he was enraged was to pray aloud for him while I was with him in his room. I didn't do this as a "strategy." I prayed because I was desperate.

Jed knew the language of privileges and consequences well. His privileges were learning to drive, summer basketball camps, overnight stays with friends, and using money he received from working or from gifts (much of that went for repairing damage he caused). We didn't use the privilege-consequence approach because someone guaranteed it would work to get and keep our kids under control. We used it because it is scriptural. But we hoped it would also "work" to help Jed think and control himself.

Connecting privileges to his choices usually did make a difference in the short run with Jed. But the water we were trying to put him in wasn't deep enough to make a lasting difference. Near the end of middle school, Betty and I met with a pastor friend and his wife, Sue, who was a Christian counselor in Philadelphia. They had had an angry and rebellious son who was deeply troubling to them, and we wanted their advice.

As Betty and I described the dynamics of Jed's influence on our two kids who still lived with us, Sue looked at us from across the table, and said, "Rick and Betty, do you know how bizarre your home life is?"

We had no idea how bad it had gotten.

We were trying to hold Jed accountable by connecting consequences and privileges to his sinful and righteous choices. But as his moods and anger escalated, we found that we had slowly accommodated in the sense that we had learned to put up with behavior we would never have allowed or tolerated in years past with our other children. Rather than address every offense, every profane word, slammed door, or angry glare, we were trying to fry the bigger fish and ended up letting the smaller ones go by. I'm not sure all of this was wrong to do, but it did leave our home with an air of tension all the time. One never knew when an explosion could occur.

Sue was right. Bizarre was the right description. We were not as serious as we needed to be about holding Jed accountable. It was like Jed was treading any water we tried to sink him in. Jed would exert his will and we would remove some privileges. Our four girls were all strong-willed too, but they responded more quickly and permanently to discipline. Jed would change his behavior for a day or two, but then he was back to display the same angry spirit.

When Jed first became a teenager Betty and I decided to be part of an African American church so that our two boys could know positive black role models rather than the criminals or professional actors or athletes that the media typically portrayed. When we started having trouble with Jed, we decided we were not going to hide the trouble we were having from the adults at school where I taught and where he was a student or from our friends at church. We were not going to gossip about Jed, but we were not going to allow this to be "our little secret." We knew we needed God's people to pray and help us—especially our black brothers and sisters from the church.

The garage incident ended, by God's mercy, with Jed putting down the gasoline and coming out of the garage. Dinner was over but so was the storm for the moment. He knew he could make different decisions because he had done so in the past. My reminder to him of some of the rich privileges that came with his good choices over the years, from my perspective, seemed to quiet his spirit. He could make good decisions, and they benefited him when he did.

Deeper Water

Only months after the garage incident Jed was caught shoplifting candy from a Seven Eleven. He had to make restitution and meet some minor legal obligations. Neither had much effect on him. Shortly after that Jed made a decision that took him into deeper water. In a fit of rage, he stormed up to his room, barricaded himself in it, and threatened to kill himself with a knife he had stolen from some place. Betty called 911.

The police came to our door, and after we explained the situation quickly, two of the officers began to climb the stairs. Jed was coming down and met them on the stairs. He had seen the flashing lights from his third floor bedroom window and wondered if the police were there for him.

"Jed, is everything all right?" the officer asked.

"Yes. I think so," he said calmly.

"Do you have a knife?"

"Yes."

"May I see it please? he asked.

Jed went to his room and got the knife.

"You were talking about hurting yourself to your parents, is that right?"

"Yeah, but I was just mad."

"Sometimes things happen to make us mad, but I think you need to come along with us right now. We're going to take you to the hospital and have you talk with a doctor over there. Your parents can come along, too."

They took Jed's knife and escorted him to their squad car. He got in the back and they took him to the psych unit of Chester-Crozier hospital about ten minutes from our home. I followed a few minutes later. When I arrived, Jed was talking to a psychiatric aide.

When Jed came out of the aide's office area into the waiting room where I was, he sat down beside me and his first words were, "Dad, that guy is not even a Christian."

"How do you know?" I asked.

"The things he was saying were crazy. He thinks you guys are the problem and not me."

The aide came over and asked to see me alone to review his observations. He urged me to have Jed admitted to the unit. I told him I appreciated his thoughtfulness and would consider it. However, I had another residential facility in mind that I researched after a meeting Betty and I had with the pastor and his counselor wife, Sue. Betty and I knew that this recommendation from the aide was exactly what the Great Physician ordered.

I had begun to research Christian residential facilities for angry, willful, defiant and violent teens. Most of them required that the teen be willing to be a resident. How were we going to persuade Jed that this is what he needed? The psychiatric aide's recommendation would give us the leverage we needed to make Jed "willing."

The next week two black pastors, a close neighbor who Jed knew and respected, and Betty and I had a surprise meeting with Jed. It was not the first time these pastors had met with Jed to warn him about the dangerous road on which he was traveling.

As the six of us met, one of the pastors took the lead. "Jed, we are here because we care about you. We've talked to you before about your behavior and how dangerous it is for you and how destructive it is for your family. It can't continue. We're here to tell you that you cannot live here any longer. Your dad and mom have found a Christian residential facility that they are going to take you to visit next week. The center will decide if they will take you, and you will decide if you are willing to go. You will either go to this ministry center or to the psych unit at the hospital, but you may not stay here any longer." Jed was speechless. This was deep water to be sure. Deeper than he had imagined. The other water that we tried to put him in was just a puddle compared to this.

The next week we did visit the ministry in Vermont. They were godly people whose mission was helping troubled youth. They interviewed and tested Jed and discussed the way the program would work. They told Jed that they could help him, but he would have to call them within the week to confirm that he wanted to come.

As we pulled out of the driveway from the main house, Jed said, "Dad, I'm not coming here!"

"The decision is yours," I said, "but weigh it carefully. You are not staying in our home. You will either be here voluntarily or you will be escorted to the psych unit at Crozier involuntarily. Those are your only options."

We traveled the eight hours home without much discussion. Jed had some thinking to do. A few days later, he called the ministry director and said he'd be willing to come.

Deepest Water

Jed spent most of his ninth grade year at the ministry center in Vermont, though he never really committed himself to the program. He had learned many good habits while in New England, but his heart was not changed. He vowed to be different if he returned home, but we were not convinced of that because his heart was the same.

The first year Jed was back was much more pleasant than before. At the end of basketball season, however, Jed decided that he didn't want to be in the Christian high school anymore. He basically stopped doing any schoolwork. The faculty agreed at the end of the year that Jed could not return. When I told Jed about the school's decision, he looked at me and said, "What am I going to do?"

I told him, "You'll be going to Chester High."

"Dad, they'll kill me there!"

"Yes, Jed, they might."

Chester High is one of the most dangerous public schools in the tri-state (Pennsylvania, Delaware and New Jersey) area. It is a tragic cesspool of drugs and violence. Many teachers mean well, but with little administrative or parent support they are mostly ineffective. The metal detectors, pat downs and chains on the main doors are symbols of the desperate conditions of the school and the community. Jed knew the condition of Chester High. We live in Chester city and he had interacted with students from there. Chester is a city that is currently ranked 84th of the top 100 most unsafe cities in the U.S.

One thing Chester High has going for it is a great basketball program. At six feet four inches, what Jed really wanted to do was play basketball. Chester has won more state championships in Pennsylvania than any other high school and is always a serious state contender. Many players from Chester get full college scholarships to Division I schools, and some make it to the pros. The head coach met Jed that summer and said he'd give him a chance to show his stuff. Chester is a bad place, but "if you stick with the basketball team, people will leave you alone," he said. Jed made the team and even started some games that fall. Then, in mid season he quit!

He and his girlfriend, Ashley, moved into someone's garage for the winter. She became pregnant and came to us for help. We allowed her to stay with us if she got back in school, but we didn't take in Jed. We couldn't handle and didn't want to enable his behavior. He slept in a Laundromat closet and ate the free meals at school.

In the early spring, Jed quit school altogether. His pregnant girlfriend went to live with her aunt and uncle in New Jersey. Jed was devastated, but he was determined to be with her.

A couple weeks later, Jed's sisters were in town and we were all getting ready to travel to our daughter's wedding in South Carolina. Jed came over to visit before we left. He was invited to the wedding but decided not to go because he had "other plans." That night he took the spare set of keys to our older second car. His scheme was to take the car to New Jersey to see Ashley and return it before we got back. The problem was he had never driven it before and had no driver's license.

When we were on the way to the wedding, about three hours south of Pennsylvania, we got a call from Jed on our cell phone.

"Dad, I'm so sorry. I'm sorry. I didn't mean for this to happen."

Jed was calling from a pay phone in Chester. He had taken our car and wrecked it before he even got out of town. He was remorseful—for the moment. After he hung up, a man drove up, put down his passenger side window and called to him, "Hey bubba, ever think of joining the army?"

"I've thought about it," Jed answered.

Sergeant Clements, also a black pastor in Chester, took Jed out for some coffee, and they talked. Their friendship began. Over the next couple of months with the help of Sergeant Clements, Jed passed the GED exam (on his first try, thanks to his earlier Christian school training), passed the physical and enlisted as an infantryman. He was just nineteen years old.

During basic training, Ashley gave birth to Julissa, a beautiful baby girl. After basic training Jed flew Ashley and Julissa to Fort Campbell in Kentucky. Jed and Ashley got married there, and the three of them moved into an apartment. Soon afterward, Jed was deployed to Iraq for fourteen months. He drove HumVees and wraparound transports.

When Jed was on leave, he loved spending time with his then eighteen-month-old daughter. He was so proud of his little girl. But his time came to return to Iraq and finish out his tour. His wife kept the apartment near Fort Campbell, but there were problems. The pressures were great for Ashley, and she got into some legal problems. She was worried that she could lose custody of their daughter, so she gave temporary custody to relatives. It turned out that the people to whom she entrusted their daughter wanted Jed out of the picture altogether. They prevented Jed from talking to his daughter on the phone and began to make plans to get court approval for full custody of her. Even Ashley didn't know about the plot to take their child. In their claim for custody, they said Ashley was an unfit mother and that Jed was an absentee dad. They made no reference to the fact that he was serving in Iraq. The water was now way over his head. Jed was gasping for breath. He was desperate. He could lose his daughter.

Through it all, ironically, Jed's affection for us never seemed to waver. He didn't like my letters to him in Iraq because he said I was preaching to him all the time, but when we did talk, he always told me he loved me. That was deeply encouraging. Now, with the threat of losing his daughter, much of his resistance to spiritual matters was beginning to melt too.

I put Jed in touch with a Christian attorney who made arrangements to work on Jed's custody case when he got out of the service. In the meantime, the lawyer informed Children and Youth Services that Jed was in the army, and they put a hold on the custody case until he was discharged.

The entire process was deeply painful to Jed. It stretched out for five or six months. The Lord knew how long Jed needed to be in the deep! For the first time, he was open to the Lord's working in his life. He talked freely about the Lord. He attended a local church near their army base and a small group Bible study with his wife. The Lord was using this pain to move him toward himself and to address the needs he and his family had.

Conclusion

In God's wonderful goodness, Jed was awarded full custody of his daughter. He and his wife are working on their marriage and the upbringing of their children (their family has expanded to include Jedidiah junior).

As you reflect on our story, keep in mind that neither Betty nor I were perfect parents through the ordeal. Oftentimes we disagreed about how to discipline Jed for his choices. We tried to keep these differences between us. (Betty usually did a better job of that than I did.) But sometimes we argued in front of the kids. I did not always control my speech and attitudes toward her. I was sometimes on edge, trying to control things that only the Lord could control. I paid the price for trying to play God more than once. On more than a few occasions I needed to ask for her and my kids' forgiveness for my sarcastic or impatient responses.

Despite our differences and arguments and not always knowing what to do, there was never a time when either of us was willing to turn away from the Lord. We tried hard to balance our many responsibilities (work, church ministries, care of our other kids, relationships with relatives and friends, and loving Jed). It was like walking a tightrope. Sometimes we fell, but by God's grace, our hearts were steadfast. We could echo David's experience in his out-of control-circumstances. He cried out to God for mercy in Psalm 57:

> Be merciful to me, O God, be merciful to me, for in you my soul takes refuge; in the shadow of your wings I will take refuge, till the storms of destruction pass by. I cry out to God Most High, to God who fulfills his purpose for me.
>
> —Psalm 57:1–2

In the midst of David's "storms of destruction" he reminded himself that the Lord's purpose would be fulfilled. There are no accidents in God's providence. Nothing about God's purpose for our family was an accident. In light of that we can say with David "My heart is steadfast, O God, my heart is steadfast! I will sing and make melody!" (Psalm 57:7).

Graciously, "his purpose" (v. 3) for us will be fulfilled, not over our dead bodies or in spite of us. But mercifully he'll do this *through* us. From eternity He created us in Christ as his workmanship, to do his good work (see Ephesians 2:10). What he has begun in us he will complete (see Philippians 1:6). This assurance allows us, like David, to exclaim, "Be exalted, O God, above the heavens! Let your glory be over all the earth!" (Psalm 57:11).

This is where God has brought Betty and me. With steadfast hearts we sing and make melody. We sing, not because there are no more heartaches (there are), not because we are perfect parents and spouses (we aren't), not because the outcomes are now settled (they're not). We sing because "God is exalted above the heavens [and his glory is] over all the earth" (Psalm 57:5). His glory is our chief delight. Nothing will prevent God from being glorified. Delighting in the Lord is the best thing for our families, our marriages and for ourselves.

> I will give thanks to you, O Lord, among the peoples;
>> I will sing praises to you among the nations.
>>> For your steadfast love is great to the heavens,
>> your faithfulness to the clouds.
>>> Be exalted, O God, above the heavens!
>> Let your glory be over all the earth!
>>>> —Psalm 57:9–11

13

WHAT WE ARE LEARNING FROM OUR PILGRIMAGE WITH AN ANGRY TEEN

The effects of an angry, defiant teen on a household are like an earthquake. It has a rippling effect from the epicenter. Not only is there the friction between the parent and the one rebelling against her authority. But an angry young person at home disturbs all surrounding relationships as well. Because of this, all of my children have read our account in the last chapter, and together we have distilled several insights. We hope these may offer some encouragement to other parents confronting the undertow forces from within themselves and rolling waves from an angry family member.

There is no special order or priority to these observations, except, perhaps, the first and last ones: pray and rejoice. If it's not obvious why these are first and last now, I hope it will be after you read about them. As I indicated in the introduction to Part Four, we can't say that we've "learned" these lessons. We're still learning. Our pilgrimage isn't finished until the Lord says it's finished, and he calls us home to be with him. But it is true that some of us have been down the path a little farther than others who are in early stages of their journey. It is our hope that counsel we are distilling from Scripture about the way our Father wants to parent an angry teen may help you to parent more wisely too.

- Pray and Weep
- Be Loving and Respectful
- Be Open to Help from Others
- Be Faithful to Other Relationships
- Seek Forgiveness
- Persevere in Hope
- Rejoice

Lesson 1: Pray and Weep

It is God who makes the water deep for each person. We need to be faithful as agents of pain, but God alone can change our teen's heart. Therefore, we need to be in serious prayer for our teens. Ultimately, we are not in control of them. Nothing convinces us of that more than times of family crisis. We can't "make" our young adults do anything. We can make life uncomfortable for them and try to put them into deep-water settings. God requires us to do so as part of his plan for us to "bring them up in the discipline and instruction of the Lord" (Ephesians 6:4). It is only God, though, who turns our teen's heart toward him. He does it with kings (see Proverbs 21:1), and he can do it with our teen anarchists.

It's not more convincing words or great signs that they need to hear or see. It is not your ability to say things just the right way or use exactly the right illustrations or the ability to logically connect with your teen's thinking that will ultimately get the point across to him. We will never be perfect parents who communicate perfectly, showing our teen just the right sense of empathy, love or respect. An angry teen will seize on our imperfections, throw them back in our faces and use them as an excuse for his angry words and actions no matter how careful we are to communicate well. This doesn't mean we should be careless about our communication. We've made that point earlier. But just as importantly, we must not think our success with our teen will be due to our rightly crafted words and body language. We need to use our understanding but not "lean" on it (Proverbs 3:5).

Jesus made it clear that not even miracles, by themselves, will send a converting message to people. In the parable of Lazarus and the rich man in Luke 16, we see that Lazarus was dropped at the rich man's gate daily hoping for crumbs to eat. Father Abraham told the rich man that there was no point in sending Lazarus back, as he was requesting, to warn his loved ones about eternal punishment. He said, "If they do not hear Moses and the Prophets, neither will they be convinced if someone should rise from the dead" (Luke 16:31). Your most perfect presentation can't change your teen's heart. The same truth is illustrated in Acts 14. The people of Lystra saw a crippled man healed and leaping and walking. Rather than the miracle bringing them to repentance and faith in Christ, when Paul and Barnabas insisted that the miracle occurred it was because of Jesus' power and not theirs, the people were easily persuaded to stone Paul. His message didn't fit their religious worldview. Even a miracle didn't convince them. Paul reminds us that we water and plant but "only God . . . gives the growth" (1 Corinthians 3:7). Our most effective work will be done on our knees.

Boldly and expectantly approach this ministry with your teen having prayed for the Spirit of God's work in and through you. Plan several seasons of prayer with your church small group, Elders, spouse or others as you begin to think about addressing these matters God's way. Consider fasting and prayer. Give focused, intense effort to the work of prayer. It is not easy, will never be convenient and will always affect you and others for whom you pray. "You have not because you ask not."

> He who goes out weeping, bearing the seed for sowing, shall come home with shouts of joy, bringing his sheaves with him.
> —Psalm 126:5–6

> Open your mouth wide, and I will fill it.
> —Psalm 81:10

Read these verses in their contexts and allow God's encouraging word to wash over you and motivate you to seek him heartily for your teen and the other members of your family.

Lesson 2: Affirm Your Love and Respect

Keep affirming your love and acceptance of your teen, regardless of his hatred or hateful acts. Therefore acknowledge your love for Christ's sake! Love does not mean approval. It means care, sacrificial giving, inconvenient service and wounding or afflicting someone for their benefit. It's all the things God's love does for his people. It also means to be encouraging in the midst of afflicting and disciplining.

As you approach your teen to talk about his attitudes or behaviors, remember that you can appreciate the fact that he is created in God's image and you can respect him for that. If there is a dark mark or smudge on a white poster board, our eyes will go to the mark or smudge. We're quick to see flaws. The same is true with what gets our attention with our angry teens.

To be sure there are lots of marks and smudges to see. I'm not trying to minimize that reality. But even in the midst of the rebellion your teen still makes some good choices—bathing, using deodorant, getting dressed, going to school, talking politely to the neighbor (even if he doesn't talk that way to you or his siblings), and many other small choices. These may seem like petty choices and praising your teen for making them may seem patronizing. However, it's important to reinforce the fact that while he's made some very hurtful and damaging decisions, he has also made good ones and continues to do so. God has given him the capacity to make choices by virtue of being created in his image. He can make good ones and you recognize that, even if his hateful and hurtful ones erupt in your home. Remind him of it.

This does not mean that you should ignore his offenses or sins. Love does not enable sin and foolishness. Neither does it hold grudges, lock a person into past failures or deny the pain caused by those failures. The love found in 1 Corinthians 13 is the familiar profile of the love our Father wants us to display to others whether they are brothers and sisters or enemies—even if it is our teen.

Affirming your love throughout the rough seas keeps the doors of communication open so that if the prodigal wants to return he feels like he has a way to do that. Let your teen know often that he is accepted and loved because Christ has accepted you. "Be kind to one another, tenderhearted, forgiving one another, *as God in Christ forgave you*" (Ephesians 4:32, emphasis mine).

Lesson 3: Be Open to Help from Others

Keep alert to what is not having the desired effect and seek counsel to take your teen into deeper water. Be open to help! God's plan has always been for his people to be part of a community of believers. "For the body does not consist of one member but of many" (1 Corinthians 12:14). None of us are self-sufficient or "independently wealthy" in the spiritual and social sense. We were created to be linked to others in God's spiritual family.

Betty and I were slow learners about what was *not* working in our efforts to apply biblical principles of discipline to Jed. It was the outside perspective of the pastors and friends we sought out that moved our thinking in new, deeper-water directions. These newer accountability measures included more pain for Jed and for us. But it also yielded some fruit that we were not expecting. God even used the non-Christian police, jailers, psychiatrists, teachers and bill collectors to make an impression on Jed that we were not able to make. God can use all kinds of people to accomplish his purposes. He used uninformed, judgmental counselors in Job's life (see Job 42:7), an ungodly Pharaoh's rebuke in Abram's life (see Genesis 12:17–19), ungodly sailors in Jonah's life (see Jonah 1:10) and the challenges of servant girls to affect Peter (see Luke 22:54–62). There are many more examples of God using unbelievers to get his message across to his people. He has the whole creation at his disposal and he chooses to use it to advance his Kingdom and rule in the world and in your family—even in surprising ways. When unbelieving friends or professionals suggest or produce new overwhelming depths of water for your teen, praise the Lord!

Open your hearts to trusted brothers and sisters in your church community. At the very least they can pray for you and with you. We grow in stability, Paul says, by the way the body speaks into our lives. This positions us so that we are not "tossed to and fro by the waves" (Ephesians 4:14). He refers to the mutual ministry of the body as one of listening and speaking.

> Rather, speaking the truth in love, we are to grow up in every way into him who is the head, into Christ, from whom the whole body, joined and held together by every joint with which it is equipped, when each part is working properly, makes the body grow so that it builds itself up in love.
>
> —Ephesians 4:15–16

"We're in this together!" one godly, humble, older saint reminded me when I was hesitating to speak openly to him about an offensive behavior that I thought he should consider. We need each other to handle the undertow and the waves. God "gives grace to the humble" (1 Peter 5:5).

Lesson 4: Be Faithful

As you are faithful to use painful measures with your teen, God will bless you. He will use it even though it may not be the way you think that makes sense in your teen's life at the moment. Therefore be faithful!

When Jed was placed in the Christian ministry in Vermont (our deeper-water measures), we had high hopes that God would use it in his life. He did, I'm sure, but not as deeply as we were hoping. Nevertheless, God did use Jed's absence in our lives. The Lord used that time to provide us with relief and rest. He helped us regain our spiritual joy, our marital and family balance and our broader life and ministry focus.

We had two other teens in our home while Jed was going through the more dramatic season of his life. One was three years older and one three years younger. Both were affected by Jed's outbursts and threatening actions as well as by our neglect of them because of the energy Jed drained from us.

By having Jed in a secure Christian environment away from us, we were able to begin some repair with these family members too.

Faithfulness does not mean we will see our desired outcomes come about. They may or may not in ways we see or don't see. The prophet Habakkuk modeled the kind of commitment God wants to characterize our faith. His trust in God's goodness and wisdom was during one of the bleakest hours of Israel's history. God had told the people through him that he was going to use an evil, violent, treacherous nation, Babylon, to discipline his people. Lots of loss and destruction would be involved. His faith, however, was not in what he saw or could imagine but in the character of his covenant-keeping God.

> Though the fig tree should not blossom, nor fruit be on the vines, the produce of the olive fail and the fields yield no food, the flock be cut off from the fold and there be no herd in the stalls, yet I will rejoice in the LORD; I will take joy in the God of my salvation. GOD the Lord is my strength; he makes my feet like the deer's; he makes me tread on my high places.
> —Habakkuk 3:17–19

Being faithful is not just a private, internal feeling. It is a commitment to live according to God's wise counsel, regardless of what others or even my own senses are telling me. That's what Habakkuk determined to do—even in the face of Israel's captivity and loss. Similarly, if it means confessing your own failures and affirming your identity, your teen's identity and accountability matters in ways that your young adult won't like, you'll do it because it's what your good, loving Father instructs you to do by faith. If it means taking actions that link his privileges to respectful behavior that God commands in your home, and he doesn't like your new approach, you will follow through because it's what your good, loving Father directs you to do by faith. If it means enlisting the help and counsel of others from your church, you'll do that by faith because you are part of a body of believers and your good and loving Father guides you to do this to gain a mature perspective about godly living in a broken world. One brother has said, "Faith is living like God is telling the truth." John the apostle affirmed that "this is the victory that has overcome the world—our faith" (1 John 5:4).

Lesson 5: Seek Forgiveness

You will sin against your teen. Therefore ask your teen's forgiveness! Your teen is not the only sinner in your household. Most of us who have acting out teens know that we've also lost control and said things out of our frustration and anger that we shouldn't have. We need to be quick to ask forgiveness not just from God but from those we offend, even our defiant teen. It is humbling, but it is also a critical part of godly parenting to confess our sins to our children when we sin against them. And to be sure, we do. The only person in your home who may be fooled into thinking that you are not offensive and do not become sinfully angry or frustrated is you.

God may use your time of confession to open doors of communication. Confession of our sins is necessary because it is right, regardless of the effect it produces. Jesus said confession should even take precedence over worship. "So if you are offering your gift at the altar and there remember that your brother has something against you, leave your gift there before the altar and go. First be reconciled to your brother, and then come and offer your gift" (Matthew 5:23–24). Jesus then goes on to say how not working to reconcile our offenses will lead to other more serious reactions that are outside of our control. What you can control is confession. What you cannot control is your teen's response. But what Jesus says in this passage is that by neglecting efforts of reconciliation, the situation will certainly deteriorate and become more desperate. "Come to terms quickly with your accuser while you are going with him to court, lest your accuser hand you over to the judge, and the judge to the guard, and you be put in prison. Truly, I say to you, you will never get out until you have paid the last penny" (Matthew 5:25–26).

The principle that we must not miss in Jesus' teaching is to do what we can to reconcile with those we've sinned against, including our teen. To avoid doing this because it is uncomfortable or because your teen was wrong too or because he may mock your words and hold it against you is beside the point. To leave an offense unconfessed is to court even more bitterness. "Whoever conceals his transgressions will not prosper, but he who confesses and forsakes them will obtain mercy" (Proverbs 28:13).

Of course your confession does not mean that your teen will necessarily respond with respect and appreciation for your humility. He may even use your confession to say "I told you so" or some other vindictive expression. Your responsibility is to confess your sin because your good and loving Father has directed you to do so. At the very least it will help you remove any logs from your own eye so that you can see the speck in your teen's eye more clearly (see Matthew 7:1–5).

More than that, though, your obedience glorifies God and will be blessed by him. "But the one who looks into the perfect law, the law of liberty, and perseveres, being no hearer who forgets but a doer who acts, he will be blessed in his doing" (James 1:25).

Lesson 6: Persevere in Hope

Once is not usually enough. Don't be discouraged if you must keep reminding your teen that the reason she is experiencing loss is because she has chosen it. It's not you "doing it to her!" You've made it plain that her angry behavior has set into motion your faithful efforts to hold her accountable. Her losses are *her* losses by her choices. Likewise, her wise choices will set into motion greater opportunities in the form of privileges.

When Change Is Very Slow

Remember, that over time your teen may have learned the patterns of behavior that have helped her get what she wants when she wants it. It may take a while for her to be convinced that the ways she's reacted in the past are not working any longer. She may need to experience the pain of going under in very deep water before she gets the message.

Pain is the tool the Lord uses to cause us to grow. The pain from our trials makes us "mature and complete, not lacking anything" (James 1:4, NIV). The writer of Hebrews said that "all discipline seems painful rather than pleasant, but later it yields the peaceful fruit of righteousness to those who have been trained by it" (Hebrews 12:11). He's your truest model. Persevere in your imitation of him.

It's easy to want what is pleasant, peaceful, enjoyable and respectable in the eyes of others. This is especially true with what goes on in a home with an angry teen. It's not wrong to want these wonderful conditions to be true. It is wrong, however, to demand that God make it so!

We can neither control the decisions our teen makes nor see the future into which God will lead them or our family. Saints through the centuries have been baffled by God's sovereign provision and pilgrimage for their families.

Who could have predicted that Tamar, daughter–in-law to Judah, the son of Jacob, would be in the line of Messiah? She pretended to be a prostitute and seduced Judah who was looking for sexual gratification. She had twin sons by him, one of whom would be included in the genealogy of the Messiah (see Genesis 38 and Matthew 1:3).

For all his godliness, David, the man after God's own heart, committed murder and adultery (for which he was deeply repentant), had a son guilty of rape and another who incited rebellion in Israel and tried to kill him (see 2 Samuel 13–15). On the other hand, Josiah, the grandson of Manasseh and the son of Amon, one of the most ungodly leaders of Israel, was one of the most godly kings to reign in Judah (see 2 Chronicles 33, 34).

None of these stories of imperfect parents give us reason to be casual about our parenting. Neither do they leave us hopeless with our own teen. The Lord is able to bring about transformation in any person. Our calling is to be faithful to bring up our children "in the discipline and instruction of the Lord" (Ephesians 6:4). This statement is in the present tense; it's in an active voice and imperative mood, which just means that it is to be a continuous (not a once and done) activity, something we must take the initiative to do (it won't happen by itself) and a role we are commanded to fulfill (it's not a suggestion). Remember, "only God . . . gives the growth" (1 Corinthians 3:7). We may think that change can't happen or that there is no hope, but God's plan oftentimes is different than ours. We need to remain faithful and persevere.

When There Are Relapses

Some time ago, Penn State University and Michigan were in a football match-up. My one son-in-law Paul is an avid Michigan fan. I vigorously root for PSU. At half time Penn State was leading by more than twenty points. I called and gloated about the shellacking that Michigan was getting. Paul's response was, "It ain't over till it's over." He was so right. The second half saw PSU collapse and Michigan do nothing wrong. They beat PSU by more than a touchdown.

Practicing deep-water principles with your teen will often result in positive movement toward respectful and responsible behavior and attitudes. But the first steps of a journey are not the same as arriving at the journey's destination. Beginning well does not guarantee one will finish that way. Give thanks to God. Enjoy and compliment changes that you see, but recognize that "it ain't over till it's over."

The counsel of God's Word urges us to make some hard decisions for our teen's benefit and for our Father's glory. We may have the temptation to expect our obedience to result in quick and significant changes. This may happen. It can if, by God's grace, our teen humbles himself and wants to change. But while we pray and hope for change by faith, we must not allow successes, however small or large, to shift our focus from our Father's will to our own strategies. "Let anyone who thinks that he stands take heed lest he fall" (1 Corinthians 10:12). The temptation to fall into self-confidence is always nearby. In another context of personal temptation, Paul asserted that when he wanted to do "right, evil lies close at hand" (Romans 7:21). It's easy to shift our confidence from a commitment to our Father's will to confidence in our own efforts when we think we see our teen respond to our discipline.

As we have seen earlier, the epitaph that can and will be written as a memorial for all the events of our days—the enjoyable ones and the hard ones—is "good" (see Romans 8:28), whether it feels that way or not. Our Father is good and does good. He is wise and sovereignly dispenses his good, wise care through the events of our days. "In your book were written, every one of them, the days that were formed for me, when as yet there were none of them" (Psalm 139:16).

When there are relapses in your teen's behavior, after he's begun to show some positive signs of growth, submission, respect and cooperation, continue to trust your Father. Continue your faithfulness. Trust in your Father's good, wise, loving care. Trust in the soundness of his promises to not allow his Word to return void. "It shall accomplish that which I purpose, and shall succeed in the thing for which I sent it" (Isaiah 55:11).

Lesson 7: Rejoice

This lesson takes us back to the focus in the introduction to Part Four. Keep your rejoicing in the Lord. Even when it looks like there isn't any hope keep rejoicing in the Lord. He will be glorified. Therefore rejoice!

This lesson summarizes many of the threads of counsel already cited in this chapter and the previous ones. The commands and counsel in the passages below are not pipedreams. They are not idealistic or sentimental platitudes from armchair theologians. They are not written for the perfect home, perfect parents or perfect

Christians. They are for believing parents who are pilgrims in a broken world, who are broken travelers with fellow broken family members. These encouragements from the Word of God are for parents in the middle of painful trials with their angry or defiant teen.

"Count it all **joy**."
 —James 1:2

These are the words of James the half brother of the Lord Jesus (see John 7:3–5). He knew suffering, having at first mocked Jesus he later saw him crucified. He knew personal failure and loss.

"Though the fig tree should not blossom, nor fruit be on the vines, the produce of the olive fail and the fields yield no food, the flock be cut off from the fold and there be no herd in the stalls, **yet I will rejoice** in the LORD; I will **take joy** in the God of my salvation. GOD, the Lord, is my strength; he makes my feet like the deer's; he makes me tread on my high places."
 —Habakkuk 3:17–19

Habakkuk's testimony and counsel for us was written as he saw his people, Israel, afflicted by ungodly enemies. He had no comfort in the prospect of any quick recovery for them. Yet his joy was in his covenant-keeping and loving God from whom he derived strength and stability.

"For we do not want you to be ignorant, brothers, of the affliction we experienced in Asia. For we were so utterly burdened beyond our strength that we despaired of life itself. Indeed, we felt that we had received the sentence of death. But that was to make us rely not on ourselves but on God who raises the dead. He delivered us from such a deadly peril, and he will deliver us. On him we have set our hope that he will deliver us again."
 —2 Corinthians 1:8–10

Paul's "sentence of death" was more than most of us will experience. However, it is not unusual for us to feel despair about what is happening to our families when an angry teen is in control.

Paul's confidence was in the "God who raises the dead." The text does not explicitly say that he was joyful, but that is not hard to surmise. "He delivered us from such a deadly peril," he said. Hope, at least, was fueled by his reliance upon God and what he saw God doing in his life. Joy must not have been far behind. Allow your confidence to be in the "God who raises the dead." He can do that in your teen, in your own personal life and in your family.

> But now thus says the Lord, he who created you, O Jacob, he who formed you O Israel: "Fear not, for I have redeemed you; I have called you by name, you are mine. When you pass through the waters, I will be with you; and through the rivers, they shall not overwhelm you; when you walk through fire you shall not be burned, and the flame shall not consume you. For I am the LORD your God, the Holy One of Israel, your Savior."
>
> —Isaiah 43:1–3

Isaiah, like Habakkuk who came after him, saw the threat to Israel because of their defiance of the LORD, not unlike the defiance of your teen. He is not merely rejecting you, he is rejecting God and his ways. But Isaiah found confidence in the LORD, the name God gave to himself as our covenant-keeping God. Allow these times to reinforce your hope—in Christ and his blood-sealed promise to you. Like Isaiah's counsel to God's people twenty-seven hundred years ago, you need not fear. God hasn't changed. His promise never fails. You will not be overwhelmed by waves and turbulence. Enjoy your security and stability in Christ.

> "You prepare a table before me in the presence of my enemies; you anoint my head with oil; my cup overflows. Surely goodness and mercy shall follow me all the days of my life, and I shall dwell in the house of the LORD forever."
>
> —Psalm 23:5–6

This beautiful Psalm was not written only for sheep lying beside quiet waters. For certain, that is the disposition that he is able to give to his people who are in the presence of their enemies.

He'll give you quietness and calmness, security in knowing that you are invited to his banquet table, which affirms you are where God wants you to be right now. His cup overflows with his joy, his provision, his contentment and his presence.

Right now, your teen may position himself as your enemy. He may say he hates you, hates your God, hates the family and even hates his own life. These are strong and passionate words. They hurt deeply. They are not the last word, however—either for him or for your hope. Trust your Good Shepherd. Allow his presence to be your joy as David asserted it to be so in many other places as well. "You make him glad with the joy of your presence" (Psalm 21:6).

DEEP, DEEPER OR DEEPEST WATER

YOU MUST TAKE ACTION

Anger is murder! Something is dying in your home if an angry teen lives there.

Your relationship with the angry teen is already on the ropes. Your marriage is tense. Your relationships with other children in the family are strained or deeply hindered by this angry presence. And your own personal physical, spiritual and emotional health is at risk.

Your angry teen is like an elephant in the living room. Your problem isn't so much that there is an elephant in the living room; your problem is getting it out. Your testimony is not in jeopardy because there *is* an elephant in the room; your testimony is in jeopardy when he's left to roam around trampling on whatever gets in his path.

The gospel of the Kingdom is a message of Christ's rule, the defeat of his enemies and the joy of his subjects. He must rule till he puts all enemies under his feet, Paul says (see 1 Corinthians 15:25). He is not surprised to find them in our homes. "A person's enemies will be those of his own household" (Matthew 10:36). The gospel's demand for submission to Christ and Christ's appointed agents (parents, pastors, civil authorities and others designated by them) cuts across the willfulness of arrogant teens. Anger flares. Murder follows.

The gospel is the power of God for salvation (see Romans 1:16). *Salvation* is a big word. It doesn't mean simply "getting saved." Paul's point is that everything sin has turned upside down, the gospel of God's grace in Christ can turn right side up again. All of life has been affected by sin and can be renovated by the gospel, including the lives of angry, murderous teens (and adults). Jesus died for sinners and invites all to come to him with their anger, pride, hurt, frustration, violence and guilty self-centeredness. He invites all who are weary and heavily burdened to come to him and find rest for their souls. The physical troubles of life might not change radically. But the spiritual life of the troubled teen or adult will come to rest.

> Come to me, all who labor and are heavy laden, and I will give you rest. Take my yoke upon you, and learn from me, for I am gentle and lowly in heart, and you will find rest for your souls. For my yoke is easy, and my burden is light.
>
> —Matthew 11:28–30

This invitation is to everyone: angry teens and hurting parents, unbelievers, new believers and long time believers. All have the same invitation. It never gets old. Come to Christ with a heart of humility and submission to do his will. His yoke is easy and his burden is light—much easier and lighter than the heaviness of living with anger, defiance, disrespect and contempt in your home.

Reread this little book and look up the passages of Scripture to read them in their context to verify that the counsel is biblical. To follow the advice offered here will involve a cost. You want to be sure, therefore, that you are following sound, biblical counsel. To do nothing will involve even more of a cost to you, your family, your teen and many others with whom you all have contact.

His yoke is easy and his burden is light! You will find rest for your soul!

HELPFUL REMINDERS

Introduction: So What's a Christian Parent to Do?

1. Don't first ask: "What should I <u>do</u> in these difficult situations?"
2. First ask: "What's a Christian parent to <u>be like</u>"

PART 1: Keeping Your Footing in Rough Waters

3. Thank your Father: for not being surprised by a home with an angry teen and imperfect parents.

Chapter 1—Keeping Your Footing as God's Glory Motivates You

4. Commit yourself first to seeking God's glory in your difficult home setting regardless of the outcome.

Chapter 2—Keeping Your Footing as God's Promises Encourage You

5. Remember the Father's promises:
   a. to be your advocate
   b. to give you wisdom
   c. to work all in your household for your good

Chapter 3—Keeping Your Footing as God's Word Instructs You

6. Trust the Word of God as:
   a. The Sword,
   b. The Lamp,
   c. The Bread,
   d. The Firm Foundation you need for parental guidance with your angry teen.

Chapter 4—Keeping Your Footing as Prayer Positions You

7. Plan special times for serious, focused prayer:

a. that you would pursue God's glory first and
b. put your trust in his good promises and wise counsel.

PART 2—Shepherding Your Teen into Deep Waters

8. Be confident that your riptide can be used by God in your home.

Chapter 5—The Riptide of Your Parental Identity

9. Acknowledge your parental sins and failures:
   a. Confess them as such to your teen
   b. Commit to being the parent God has appointed you to be –for his Glory

Chapter 6—The Riptide of Your Teen's Identity

10. Affirm your teen's young adult status:
    a. Include his ability to make choices
    b. Choices have consequences

Chapter 7—The Riptide of Accountability

11. Understand God's design that parental love and painful discipline are companions.

PART 3—Allowing Your Teen to Sink in Deep Waters (Sinking Is Not Drowning)

12. Consider how you may use "deep water" as a means of God's gracious work in your angry teen.

Chapter 8—Make the Water Deep: By Differentiating Privileges and Rights

13. Differentiate Privileges and Rights:
    a. Privileges are usually attached to our choices
    b. Privileges most often forfeited by foolishness

Chapter 9—Make the Water Deeper: By Attaching Privileges to Respectful and Responsible Choices

14. Focus on:
    a. How teens gain or give up privileges
       1. Based upon his choices
    b. His decisions, not yours, determine what he enjoys or suffers

Chapter 10—Make the Water Deepest: By Identifying Respectful and Responsible Attitudes

15. Attitudes:
    a. Are choices about communication
    b. Produce privileges or losses just as actions do

Chapter 11—Develop Your Plan to Shepherd Your Teen into Deep Water

16. Pray
17. Prioritize your expectations
18. Create a two-week plan
19. Explain plan to your teen

PART 4—Our Story – "You Have Made Him Glad with the Joy of Your Presence"

20. Trust your Father to be at work in your home situation as he is in authors

Chapter 12—Deep, Deeper and Deepest Water in Our Household

21. Be faithful through your tears
22. Be joyful in your hope!

Chapter 13—What We Are Learning from Our Pilgrimage with an Angry Teen

23. Be teachable through your parenting pilgrimage.

Conclusion—Deep, Deeper or Deepest Water: You Must Take Action

24. Accept Jesus' invitation to:
    a. Come to him
    b. Take up his yoke
    c. Learn from him
    d. He offers rest to every parent and teen who does this—regardless of the painful situation.

NOTES

1. "Pier Hell: Anatomy of a Disaster," Maralyn Lois Polak, World Net Daily, May 24, 2000, www.wnd.com/news/article.asp?ARTICLE_ID=19987.

2. A note on Proverbs 1:7 by Charles Bridges, *A Commentary on Proverbs*, pp. 3,4. Banner of Truth Trust, London, First published 1846, First Banner of Truth Trust edition, 1968.

3. Bruce, K. Waltke, *The Book of Proverbs, Chapters 1–15*. (Grand Rapids: William B. Eerdmans Publishing Company, 2004), 174–176.

4. Bruce Waltke, 574.

5. David and Phyllis York, *Toughlove* and *Toughlove Solutions*. (New York: Bantam Books, 1983).

6. Derek Kidner, *The Proverbs, An Introduction and Commentary*. (Downers Grove, Illinois: InterVarsity Press, 1977), p. 83.

7. Bruce Waltke, 442–443.

8. This theme is developed more thoroughly in my companion to this book, *Get Outta My Face* (Wapwallopen, PA: Shepherd Press, 2009) and is the entire theme of my book for Christian educators *Scorners and Mockers: How to Dampen Their Influence in Your School* (Colorado Springs: Purposeful Design, 2004).

9. Jed and our other adult children have read these accounts and have given permission to make reference to them. At this writing our adult children range from 20 to 36 years of age. Jed is number five of the six and the oldest of our two adopted boys.

SCRIPTURE INDEX

Mark
7:20–23
9:24

Luke
5:32
6:28
15:13
15:17
16:31

John
3:16
3:20
4:15
6:35
6:48–56, 58, 63
6:51
6:66
7:17
8:31–32
10:10
11:4
11:21
11:35
11:40
15:2
16:12
16:13
16:33
17:17

Acts
9:1

Romans
2:13–16
2:13–16
3:23
5:12
6:23

7:15–19
7:21

8:1–2
8:18
8:28
8:32
8:37–40
8:39
9:1–5; 22–26;
    11:1–7; 25–27
9:2
10:9
10:17
11:33, 36
11:26

1 Corinthians
1:17
1:28–29
3:7
11:30
10:6–11
10:12
12:14

2 Corinthians
1:8–10
12:7–10
12:9

Galatians
1:8
5:19–21
5:19–23 (ESV,
    NIV)
6:7–8

Ephesians
4:32
4:14

4:15–16
6:4
6:13–14
6:10
6:18

Philippians
1:6
1:29
2:7
2:10–11
3:8–14

Colossians
1:20
3:21

2 Timothy
2:19
3:17

2 Thessalonians
3:10

Hebrews
4:12
4:1–2
4:15–16
9:14
12:1–5
12:6
12:5–11
12:11
13:20–21

James
1:2
1:4
1:2–4
1:5–8
1:17

1:25
2:10
3:17
4:8
4:6
4:2
5:16–18

1 Peter
1:15–16
1:23; 2:2
4:1–2
5:5
5:9–11

2 Peter
1:3
1:4
1:19

1 John
1:7
1:8, 10
1:9
2:1–2
3:2
3:2–3
3:3
5:4

Jude
24–25

Revelation
7:9–12, 14, 17